CHRISTOINTEGRATION

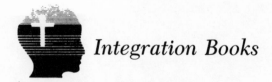

Integration Books

STUDIES IN PASTORAL PSYCHOLOGY, THEOLOGY, AND SPIRITUALITY
Robert J. Wicks, General Editor

also in this series

CHRISTOINTEGRATION

*The Transforming Love
of Jesus Christ*

by
Bernard J. Tyrrell

Integration Books

paulist press/new york/mahwah

Imprimi Potest

David Leigh, S.J.
Censor, Oregon Province of the Society of Jesus

Library of Congress Cataloging-in-Publication Data

Tyrrell, Bernard, 1933-
   Christointegration: the transforming love of Jesus Christ/by
Bernard J. Tyrrell.
     p. cm.—(Integration books)
    Bibliography: p.
    ISBN 0-8091-3098-X: $9.95 (est.)
    1. Jesus Christ—Person and offices. 2. Christian life—Catholic
authors. I. Title. II. Series.
BT202.T897   1989
248.4'82—dc20   89-35834
                                           CIP

Published by Paulist Press
997 Macarthur Boulevard
Mahwah, New Jersey 07430

Printed and bound in the
United States of America

Contents

In Loving Memory of
Sister Elizabeth Clare Tyrrell, S.P.
and
Fr. Terry Koreski

Foreword

In *Christotherapy* and *Christotherapy II* Bernard Tyrrell beautifully emphasized and brought new light to the presence in our lives of Jesus as healer. In his new work, *Christointegration: The Transforming Love of Jesus Christ*, he moves this focus forward by focusing on the theme: "the inner experience of the consoling, inspiring, life-giving love of Jesus Christ."

How Bernard Tyrrell tells us his views is just as important as what he presents to us. In *Christointegration* he reveals that "The love of Christ 'impels' (2 Cor 5:14) me to seek to share my joy in his love with others." As you experience his book, you can *feel* this. His heart fills the pages just as much as his ideas do. His spirit guides us toward a deeper integration in our lives as much as his reflections do.

Ever practical in his questions to the reader, his queries are simple, reflective and the obvious fruit of his own daily vibrant personal consciousness examens. Thoroughly scriptural in context, there are ample biblical citations to enrich the reflection on the ideas and approaches he offers.

In *Christointegration* the "ongoing affair of heart, mind, and spirit" with Jesus that Tyrrell is experiencing is shared with us through imagery as well as theological and literary sources that bring his positions to life. His goal is to have us move our eyes from the heavens and to see the Lord's vital presence in our hearts and in the community of life around us. To accomplish this, he shares what he has learned from the spirit, lives and writings of such a myriad of people as Jean Vanier, Karl Rahner, Mother Teresa, Dorothy Day, Julian of Norwich, Catherine de Hueck Doherty, Oscar Romero, Bernard of Clairvaux, Charles de Foucauld, Damien of Molokai, Rosemary Haughton, Thérèse of Lisieux, and others too numerous to name in this brief introduction.

Christointegration is, in essence, a book of prayer and friend-

1

ship. It is designed to open up new dimensions in our heart so the communication we have with God can be brought forth in self-awareness/appreciation and in our interactions with others. The spirit of 2 Corinthians (1:3–6) pervades the entire book: "Blessed be the God and Father of our Lord Jesus Christ, a gentle Father and the God of all consolation, who comforts us in all our sorrows, so that we can offer others, in their sorrows, the consolation that we have received from God ourselves. Indeed, as the sufferings of Christ overflow to us, so, through Christ, does our consolation overflow." And so, the title *Christointegration* is a fitting one for this book because the focus (as named in the subtitle) "the transforming love of Jesus Christ" fills each page and calls us to a new life with God that impels us as it has and continues to impel Bernard Tyrrell to love and to love boldly.

Robert J. Wicks
Series Editor

Introduction

Love is the eye by means of which we can see that Thou art good.

—Aelred of Rievaulx

He who died for us is all that I seek; He who rose again for us is my whole desire.

—Ignatius of Antioch

It seems more than a happy coincidence that I literally completed my revision of the last chapter of this book on July 30, the eve of the feast of Saint Ignatius Loyola, and so have the added joy of the gift of composing this preface on the feast day itself. For, as a Jesuit, I know from my heart that the richest source of inspiration for this book, apart from the holy scriptures and the sacraments of the church, is the spirituality of Saint Ignatius Loyola, especially as it reveals itself in his *Spiritual Exercises.*

Ignatius of Loyola, like the early Christian martyr Ignatius of Antioch, was on fire with a passionate love of Jesus Christ and a desire to share the good news of the kingdom and of Jesus' love with others. It is this same love of Jesus and the desire to share the joy of his transforming love with others that inspired in me the desire to write this book.

Any reader of this book will inevitably find herself or himself personally faced by Jesus with three questions he asks of certain individuals in the gospels, but which are meant for all: "But who do you say that I am?" (Mt 16:15). "Do you love me?" (Jn 21:17). "Which of these three [the priest, the Levite, or the Samaritan], do you think, proved neighbor to the man who fell among the robbers?" (Lk 10:36). My tack in this book is to offer concrete examples from sacred scripture and the lives of holy people which will

3

serve as "spiritual catalysts" for evoking heartfelt answers to Jesus' questions from readers who are true "seekers" (Mt 7:8).

Two of my earlier books focused on Jesus as healer. They were forged in the crucible of my own struggles for healing and in my work—with Christ's help—for the healing of others. But I find myself more and more captivated by Jesus the life-giver, the bestower of ever more abundant life (Jn 10:10), "pressed down, shaken together, running over" (Lk 6:38). It is not that I no longer need or pray for healing—I need it and pray for it daily in all areas of my life. But I find that the more I focus on Jesus, not only as savior and healer, but also as brother, teacher, liberator, friend, beloved, lover, Lord and God, the richer life becomes and the more my consciousness is filled with a sense of peace, hope, love, joy, gratitude, assurance.

This book is the fruit of reflection and prayer and it is intended to be assimilated through prayerful reflections. It is meant for believers in Jesus Christ, but it is also written for those who are seeking, but have not yet found, a sufficiently hopeful and sustaining answer to the mystery of life. I also intend this book for spiritual directors, chaplains, pastoral counselors who are gifted by the Holy Spirit with a charism for guiding and aiding others in their quest for more abundant life and a deeper love-relationship with God. For surely anyone who feels called to assist others in the realization of an ever fuller intrapersonal and interpersonal integration in Christ and growth in friendship with Christ needs to seek constantly to respond at ever deeper levels to the three questions Jesus Christ poses to all of us.

On a very practical note, the first chapter of this book contains many practical suggestions about how best to read the following chapters, what questions to have in mind about the images of Jesus, what methods of prayer might most fruitfully be employed in reflecting on the diverse images of Jesus. Also, the references in the text itself provide a wealth of materials for further reading. Consequently, there is no need to add a further list of recommended readings.

I would like to thank most especially Dr. David Leigh, S.J., Sister Clare Lentz, S.P., Ms. Phyllis Pobst and Dr. Carolyn Thomas, S.C.N. for their careful reading of my manuscript and the many excellent suggestions they offered for improving the book. I want them to know that their help was absolutely indispensable for the successful completion of what I intended as a "labor of love" in the service of Jesus Christ, but which I slowly discovered demanded a much more strenuous kind of "labor" and a more patient, persevering "love" than I had originally anticipated.

I am also most grateful to Sister J. Bernadette Carroll, S.C., Dr. David Fleiger and Sister Honor Mounteer, S.N.J.M. for the special ways in which they helped make this book a reality. Finally, I would like to thank the members of the Jesuit community at the University of San Francisco for the gracious hospitality they showed toward me during my sabbatical year in which I wrote the present book.

Dr. Bernard Tyrrell, S.J.
July 31, 1988
Feast of Saint Ignatius of Loyola
San Francisco, California

1

Loving Jesus Christ Today

Is an intimate, loving relationship with Jesus Christ possible and desirable today? Certainly there are millions of sincere human beings throughout the world who profess a deep, personal love for Jesus Christ. The facts seem to prove the possibility of such a love. But is the investing of time and energy in fostering an intimate love relationship with Jesus Christ really desirable? Is not such an engagement essentially a self-indulgent, private affair that turns an individual inward instead of outward in an urgent concern for the oppressed, the hungry, the exploited? The facts disallow a facile "yes" response to our last question.

Experience provides us with many striking examples of individuals who profess a deep personal love for Jesus and at the same time work tirelessly in the service of the poor, the outcasts, the tortured. There is Mother Teresa, known throughout the world for her care for the dying in the slums of Calcutta and elsewhere; there is Jean Vanier, who has dedicated his whole life to the service of the mentally handicapped; there is Oscar Romero, who gave his life rather than remain silent in the face of the torture, exploitation and oppression of the innocent poor in El Salvador. It remains true, however, that even an openly professed love for Jesus Christ can be opportunistic, self-referential, egoistic to the core. The acid test of the authenticity of a personal love of Christ is the fulfillment of the criteria Jesus himself sets down: "Each tree is known by its own fruit" (Lk 6:44).

The Gospel Link of Love of God
and Love of Neighbor

Love is at the core of the revelation of Jesus Christ. But in the gospels the love of God and the love of neighbor are inseparably

7

linked together. The same is true of the love of Jesus and the love of neighbor. It is impossible genuinely to love Jesus and yet to hate one's neighbor. It is impossible to love Jesus in an authentic way and at the same time to refuse to participate in the building up of the kingdom, of the reign of God here on earth. Anyone, for example, who has sincerely participated in the *Spiritual Exercises* of Saint Ignatius knows "from the heart" that the cultivation of an intimate knowledge and love of Jesus Christ is one of the most powerful ways to dispose oneself for a passionate commitment to the quest for justice for all and peace upon earth.

Difficulties in Discovering the Most Needy Neighbor

But this reflection on the unity of the love of Jesus and the love of neighbor gives rise to a new question that we dodge only at our peril: If a person truly loves Jesus, does this mean that he or she will be able to discern without difficulty who those "neighbors" are that are most in need of assistance? The age-long struggles that disciples of Jesus have experienced in coming to recognize the enslaved, the exploited, the victims *in their very midst* make it painfully evident that an intimate love of Jesus in no way guarantees that the follower of Jesus will spontaneously recognize who those "neighbors" are that most need help. It is only through much prayer, searching of heart, and constant alertness to prophetic voices that followers of Jesus come to see who those "neighbors" are that here and now in their very midst are truly victims and most in need of assistance.

Racial and Sexual Discrimination

In the United States it was only in the second half of the twentieth century that a significant number of followers of Jesus came to recognize clearly the awful racial discrimination that they were practicing in a more or less unconscious fashion. And as this century comes to an end there remains a long, long way to go in the unmasking of more subtle forms of racism that Christians and others continue to practice.

Even more recent is the discovery on the part of many believers of diverse forms of discrimination against women that exist among believers and unbelievers alike. Indeed, the realization that even Christian churches are not free of certain forms of discrimination against women has become a source of severe scandal to some

Christians. These Christians have even been led to ask the radical question: Is it possible to love Jesus himself, since he was a male member of a patriarchal society in which discrimination against women was widespread? Happily, a growing number of biblical exegetes and other scholarly voices—both female and male—are answering this question in the affirmative. They attest that Jesus himself strongly opposed deeply embedded discriminatory practices against women[1] and that he treated women with a respect, sense of equality and friendship that shocked and angered his contemporaries.[2] This realization does not automatically solve all the problems of discrimination against women that may exist in contemporary Christian churches in one form or other, but it does provide a source of hope and a firm foundation for ultimate reform in the person and life of Jesus who is the "pioneer and perfecter of our faith" (Heb 12:2).

Stages in the Process of Discovering and Loving the Neighbor

Our reflections on the unity of the love of Jesus and the love of neighbor clearly reveal that there are stages of development in the process through which we come to discover and love our "neighbor" in Christ. Initially a person loves those who are members of his or her own family. This love gradually expands to include friends of the family, members of one's church, associates in work and play. A major breakthrough occurs when the believer comes to discover and love the "neighbor" in the poor, the alienated, the disadvantaged in his or her own community. Another great leap forward takes place when the follower of Jesus becomes truly concerned about all suffering human beings who live in the "global village" we call earth. Of course, no one can concretely aid every human being who suffers anywhere. But through the exercise of civic responsibilities such as voting, by joining at least one group that works for such a cause as the alleviation of world hunger, the freeing of prisoners of conscience, or the defense of human rights wherever they are violated, the believer is transformed into a person who feels a kinship with all those who suffer anywhere in the world. In this case there is no need to choose between an intimate, loving relationship with Jesus and service of the poor, the enslaved, all who suffer. In fact, intimacy with Jesus becomes an inward dynamo, a fiery love that opens the heart to the embrace and service of all who are in need.

Why Relate to Jesus Rather Than Just to "God"?

Yet, if I am a believing Christian but do not enjoy an intimate love relationship with Christ, why is this so? Do I perhaps believe that it is enough to love God, since the whole point of Jesus' life, death and resurrection is to lead us to the one he speaks of as "my God and your God" (Jn 20:17)? But is there not in the gospel of John a riveting, intensive portrayal of the intimate love relationship between Jesus and the individual believer?[3] Are there not good grounds for arguing that a personal communion in love with Jesus Christ is a fundamental dimension of the revelation in the New Testament and in the Christian tradition?[4] How is it possible for the believing Christian to resist the many invitations to love him that the gospel of John places on the lips of Jesus? "He who loves me will be loved by my Father, and I will love him and manifest myself to him" (Jn 14:21).[5] Does not Jesus' promise to reveal himself to the one who loves him stir up in the heart of the believer a burgeoning desire to say to Jesus Christ: "Here I am. You know that in the depths of my heart I desire to love you. Help me in my lack of love."

But perhaps the Christian who is well advanced in the ways of prayer might ask: Is it not the teaching of the mystics that the aim of contemplative prayer in its highest forms is to go entirely beyond the humanity of Jesus and to enter into a totally spiritual union with God who is Spirit? The great Christian mystic Teresa of Avila in her *Interior Castle*[6] strongly rejects the kind of mysticism that preaches a flight from the humanity of Jesus[7] and even affirms that one of the joys of heaven will be the lasting contemplation of Jesus in glory.[8] The theologian Karl Rahner likewise emphasizes that even after the end of history Jesus Christ, who is the same "yesterday and today and for ever" (Heb 13:8), remains the abiding ground of our immediate relationship to God in resurrected glory.[9]

The Difference Loving Jesus Makes

Even at this point some believers may still ask themselves: Why should I devote a significant amount of my prayer time to fostering an intimate love relationship with Jesus Christ? What practical difference in my life will this relationship really make?

This entire book is, in a way, an attempt to answer this question. But an initial response is appropriate. Thus, any encounter with another person makes a difference in one's life. Some encounters are vastly more important than others, but all impact on a person's individual history. Clearly, faith-encounters with Jesus Christ have made a monumental difference in the historical lives of those we call "Christian saints." Belief in Jesus Christ and love of him intoxicated the saints, transformed their consciousness, shaped their vision of life and the world and in many cases led to earth-shaking historical actions. Then there are the rest of us who believe in Jesus Christ and love him.

To any person who deeply loves Jesus Christ, the "difference" that this love makes is palpable and wonderful. For the person in love with Jesus Christ this love is just as real, just as affective, just as beautiful as any love-encounter between human beings. In fact, because Jesus is who he is, the encounter is without parallel, and more important than any other human interpersonal encounter. If it is true, for example, that any authentic human friendship changes and deeply enriches the participants in this friendship, this is even more radically the case in friendship with Jesus. The friend of Jesus can say: "My friendship with Jesus molds my perceptions of life; it colors the way I respond to situations and to other persons. My friendship with Jesus makes faith, hope and love the deepest pulsating realities in my daily living. My friendship with Jesus gives me confidence in the victory of the forces of life over the powers of darkness. My friendship with Jesus gives a deeper meaning and value to all my other friendships. My friendship with Jesus involves a whole constellation of meanings and values that provide me with a unique vision of life and eternity." In other words, loving Jesus not only "makes a difference," it "makes all the difference."

Love of Jesus Within a Community of Believers

Some might object that my impassioned defense of the unique value of a personal relationship with Jesus Christ threatens to eclipse the core reality that Christians are primarily a community of believers and not isolated individuals existing in solitary relationships with Jesus. My basic response is that generally Jesus reveals himself to contemporary persons as one who loves them through other human beings who bear witness to the love Jesus has for them and they for him.

And how are they to believe in him of whom they have never heard? And how are they to hear without a preacher? . . . As it is written: "How beautiful are the feet of them that preach good news!" (Rom 10:14–15).

Belief in Jesus as one "who loved me and gave himself for me" (Gal 2:20) occurs within a community of believers who confess that the Father of our Lord Jesus Christ "chose us in him before the foundation of the world, that we should be holy and blameless before him" (Eph 1:4). Even Saul, later Paul, to whom Jesus revealed himself in a strikingly manifest way, was sent to members of the Christian community immediately after his "encounter" with Jesus on the way to Damascus (Acts 9:1–22). The Christian community accepted Paul as one especially chosen by God to be an apostle to the Gentiles. In listing the individuals to whom Jesus appeared after his resurrection Paul ends by saying: "Last of all, as to one untimely born, he appeared also to me" (1 Cor 15:8). Every interpersonal relationship with Jesus, no matter how unique, intimate and unrepeatable, occurs within the community of believers, chosen by God before the foundation of the world. Even a person who comes to believe in Jesus Christ and love him apart from any formal membership in a Christian community is in some mysterious way related to the community of believers through the inner working of the Holy Spirit.

Yet today there are many sincere individuals who feel a certain attraction toward Jesus Christ, but find themselves incapable of believing in him. One of the most painful experiences I have had is in talking with persons who tell me they yearn to believe, but cannot, and who end the conversation by asking me, in effect, to give them the gift of belief in Jesus Christ. This is a gift no mere human can bestow. God alone grants this gift. But I tell sincere seekers that their very desire to believe is already evidence of God's Holy Spirit at work within their hearts. I suggest to them that they should, above all, seek to be true to their consciences and to strive to live in intelligent, reasonable, responsible and loving ways. I also advise that they read holy scripture and the lives of the saints, and that they talk with holy people who love Jesus Christ. If it seems appropriate, I also counsel that they attend religious services and perhaps make some kind of Christian "retreat" or spiritual exercises. Finally, I urge that they seek especially to be attentive to the inspirations of the "still, small voice" of God within the heart. If they do these things, they need have no fear that God has abandoned or forsaken them. For God is mysteriously at work through the Holy Spirit of Christ, transforming the hearts of all human beings of good will, even though most may not know this in an explicit way.

Core Beliefs Grounding a Prayer-Relationship with Jesus

But here the focus is on those who do believe. Our reflections center on the believer's personal love of Jesus Christ and the transformation this love effects in the one who loves. It is helpful here to express in very simple terms those core beliefs concerning Jesus that the believer needs to profess from the heart in order to participate as richly as possible in an intimate, ongoing, loving encounter with him.

Jesus Is Alive in the Glory of God the Father

The follower of Jesus, first of all, needs to be able to say to him:

I believe, Jesus, that you, who were born of a woman (Gal 4:4), lived a human life, suffered and died for the salvation of all human beings (2 Cor 5:14), have been raised from the dead (Rom 6:9) and are now and forever alive in the glorious presence of God (Rev 1:17–18).

The ringing affirmation that Jesus of Nazareth is risen from the dead and alive forever in the presence of the Father is at the very core of the good news. In the gospel of John in the early morning of the day of resurrection Jesus tells his beloved Mary Magdalene to "go to my brethren and say to them, I am ascending to my Father and your Father, to my God and your God" (Jn 20:17). Luke renders testimony to the abiding presence of the risen Jesus with the Father in his description of the martyrdom of Stephen:

But he, full of the Holy Spirit, gazed into heaven and saw the glory of God, and Jesus standing at the right hand of God and he said, "Behold, I see the heavens opened, and the Son of Man standing at the right hand of God" (Acts 7:55–56).

Likewise, the author of the book of Revelation writes of a vision he had on the Lord's day in which Jesus said to him: "I am the first and the last, and the living one; I died, and behold I am alive forever more . . ." (Rev 1:17–18).

Christ Is Present to All in Knowing and Loving Them

The belief that Jesus is alive now is an absolute precondition for any possibility of a dynamic, ongoing interchange of love, between the believer and Jesus. But it is not enough that Jesus is alive. He must also be present in knowledge and love to the believer. This means that the follower of Jesus must also be able to say to him in living faith:

> I believe, Jesus, that here and now you are more intimately present in knowledge and love to me and all human beings than we are to ourselves in the very depths of our being.

There is a striking, no doubt intentional, parallel between Luke's portrayal of Jesus' last words on the cross and his account of the final words of Stephen as his persecutors were stoning him to death. About Jesus in his dying moment Luke writes, "Then Jesus, crying with a loud voice, said, 'Father, into thy hands I commit my spirit' " (Lk 23:46). Similarly, Luke writes about Stephen's final moments of life: "And as they were stoning Stephen, he prayed, 'Lord Jesus, receive my spirit' " (Acts 7:59). Clearly, Luke, in his dramatic account of the words of the dying Stephen, is expressing a fundamental belief of the early Christians that the risen Jesus was intimately present to all of his people in knowledge and love. The gospel of John is perhaps most explicit about the abiding love of Jesus for all his people. The evangelist puts on the lips of Jesus the promise that after his departure he will not leave his disciples desolate, but will come to them (Jn 14:18). Indeed, Jesus says that "if a man loves me, he will keep my word, and my Father will love him, and we will make our home with him" (Jn 14:23). The gospel of John is permeated with a sense of the intimacy in knowledge and love that exists between Jesus and the believer.

He Always Lives To Make Intercession

Each believer can properly take as addressed to herself or himself the words of Jesus: "I am the good shepherd; I know my own and my own know me" (Jn 10:14). But it is not sufficient for the fullness of a love relationship with Jesus that he be alive in glory and know and love the believer. The deepest nature of love impels the lover to be intimately involved in the life of the beloved; it requires that the lover bestow gifts and perform "labors of love" for the one loved; it demands that the lover always seek to bring good in some fashion or other to the one loved, even in the most difficult of circumstances. This means that the one whom Jesus loves should be able to say to him with the deep trust of a living faith:

> I believe, Jesus, that you are daily active, working, interceding, seeking to bring good out of all the events of my life and the lives of all who in the hidden recesses of their hearts are open to you—whether they realize it or not.

In the calling of Saul we have a striking example of a direct intervention of the risen Jesus in the life of an individual. Saul, on his way to Damascus, was "waylaid" by Jesus, who said to him: "I am Jesus, whom you are persecuting" (Acts 9:5). Saul was sent to Ananias who said to him: "Brother Saul, the Lord Jesus who appeared to you on the road by which you came, has sent me that you may regain your sight and be filled with the Holy Spirit" (Acts 9:17).

Throughout the history of the Christian church countless individuals have experienced Jesus at work in their lives in varying degrees of intensity. In some cases, the interventions were highly dramatic. Saint Ignatius of Loyola had a number of vivid, mystical encounters with Jesus. Ignatius experienced Jesus as presenting prayers he was offering to the Father,[10] as giving him inner strength and assurance in a major decision he was called to make.[11] In commenting on such experiences Ignatius wrote: "At these times, when I sensed or saw Jesus, I felt so great a love within me that I thought nothing could happen in the future that would separate me from Him . . ."[12]

Certainly Jesus does at times intervene in the lives of individuals by granting them special visions for the accomplishment of unique missions. But Jesus most often reveals himself to believers as active in their lives through the discerning eye of faith, rather than in visions. Paul writes: "We know that in everything God works for good with those who love him, who are called according to his purpose" (Rom 8:28). But in John Jesus says: "My Father is working still, and I am working" (Jn 5:17). If both the Father and Jesus come to dwell in the person who loves Jesus, it must certainly be true that both the Father and Jesus are working for good in everything with those who love them. Also, there is the image of Jesus presented to us in Hebrews: "[Jesus] holds his priesthood permanently, because he continues forever. Consequently he is able for all time to save those who draw near to God through him, since he always lives to make intercession for them" (Heb 7:24–25). The belief that Jesus is always present, active, working, interceding, drawing good from all the events of the lives of those who love him explains the joy-filled exclamation in the first epistle of Peter: "Without having seen him you love him; though you do not now see him you believe in him and rejoice with unutterable and exalted joy" (1 Pet 1:8).

In the love-relationship between Jesus and the believer the initiative is on the side of Jesus. For this reason the follower of Jesus can transpose the famous poetic question of Elizabeth Barrett Browning and ask concerning Jesus: "How does he love me? Let me count the ways." The basic sources for discovering the ways in which Jesus loves each human being in his or her uniqueness include holy scripture, the prayers of the church in its sacraments and in the feasts it celebrates, the great professions of Christian belief, the lives and writings of the saints, the religious experience of individuals and groups, and the insights that result from the church's creative response to the questions and challenges that each new age and cultural development present.

Dynamic Interplay of Images and Feelings

The images of Jesus disclosed to us in holy scripture provide the most basic and important revelation of the ways in which Jesus loves us. The New Testament offers us a striking variety of images of Jesus. He is shepherd and he is friend; he is king and he is brother. The images of Jesus as savior, healer, liberator, brother, friend, beloved, spouse are among those that tend to evoke powerful affective responses from certain believers today. These images tend to be primal, archetypal and meaningful to individuals of highly diverse cultural backgrounds. Of course, these images do not exhaust the ways in which Jesus reveals himself to humankind nor are they of equal affective appeal to all. Like a diamond, Jesus has many facets, many ways in which he flashes forth love, beauty, fidelity, truth, wholeness, goodness, integrity. Each of the ways Jesus reveals himself has its own special meaning and value, and each way that Jesus discloses himself evokes a unique set of feelings.

The topic of feelings plays a pivotal role in this book because our primary concern is with growth in one's affective relationship with Jesus Christ and the consequent transformation of our affective relationships with one another in Christ. Of course, an affective transformation that does not manifest itself in deeds, in transformed behavior, proves itself to be a pseudo or inauthentic affective transformation.

Further, there is a powerful interconnection between feelings and images, especially such interpersonal images as savior, healer, liberator, brother, friend, beloved, lover. These latter images are alive with feeling. They evoke feelings and are evoked by feelings. As psychologist-theologian Ann Ulanov remarks: "Images—the language of the psyche—are the coin of life; they touch our emotions as well as our thoughts; they reach down into our bodies as well as toward our ideas."[13]

Kataphatic and Apophatic Approaches to God

Throughout the history of Christianity theologians have often viewed feelings with great suspicion, though there have always been those who championed the excellence and importance of feelings in human living and in spiritual development. Interestingly, the gospels are alive with images and feelings and Jesus emerges as a man of deep feelings. Experts in the history of Christian spirituality point out that an emphasis on images of God—the kataphatic approach—always found itself counterbalanced by an insistence on going beyond images—the apophatic approach. But Urban T. Holmes in his *A History of Christian Spirituality* points out that the spirituality of the New Testament is basically kataphatic and generally "more affective than speculative."[14] Consequently, my emphasis on feelings in this present work on the love of Jesus Christ should not surprise or disconcert anyone.

Hierarchy of Feelings

Of course, if a person has a reductionistic view of feelings and views them as nothing more than physiological sensations, then my stress on feelings may seem rather inappropriate in a book on the love of Jesus Christ. But if a person holds that there are various types of feelings, reaching from the most primitive bodily sensations up to the feeling state of being in love with God, then the appropriateness of my focus on feelings in reflecting on the transforming love of Jesus Christ will be quite apparent.

Some thinkers, indeed, consider feelings as nothing more than physical sensations, e.g. fatigue, excitement, pain, fear, sexual desire. But I, in agreement with philosopher Bernard Lonergan and others, view feelings as involving many qualitatively distinct forms. Certainly there exist mere physical feelings. But there are also feelings that greet, appreciate, recognize, discern and respond to values such as works of art, moral achievements, human beings in their deepest personal reality.[15] Such are the feelings that appreciatively apprehend and reveal to us in a unique way the beauty of a concerto, the grace of a ballerina, the richly diverse values of sisterly love, of motherly love, of the love of friendship and the numinous splendor of the divine mystery. Feelings that recognize the deepest human and spiritual values belong to the realm of the "heart."[16] These latter feelings belong as much to the depths of the human being as do his or her thoughts or choices.

Feelings of the Risen Jesus

Key questions at once arise about the nature of the feelings of the historical Jesus toward those whom he encountered in his earthly life and his feelings now in his resurrected state toward those living here on earth. What kind of feelings did Jesus show toward his contemporaries? Did he experience the special feelings of a brother, of a friend, of a teacher? Does Jesus continue to experience feelings in his resurrected state? If so, what kind of feelings does he experience? My aim in the chapters that follow is, in part, to show both how the historical Jesus related in his mind and heart, in his thoughts and feelings, to his contemporaries and how he has continued in his glorified state to reveal his thoughts and feelings to believers, especially to the saints. And since it is, above all, particular images and symbols that evoke feelings and are evoked by feelings, the focal point of our meditative reflections will be the primal images of Jesus as savior, healer, liberator, brother, friend, beloved, spouse.

But in this introductory chapter I would like to consider in a more global fashion the questions regarding the ways in which the risen Jesus relates to us, reveals himself to us and how he feels toward us, as those who have not seen, but yet believe (Jn 20:29).

In the middle ages theologians asked many questions about what the qualities of the resurrected body would be. Today there is more interest in the characteristics of the risen, glorified human mind, heart, psyche. For example, thinkers ask: Does the risen Jesus in his glorified human nature experience feelings as well as thoughts about those of us now living here on earth? Holy scripture in the resurrection accounts presents us with the risen Jesus who asks Simon Peter a number of times: "Do you love me?" (Jn 21:15–17). Jesus is also portrayed as calling Mary Magdalene by name (Jn 20:16–18) in a way that evokes powerful feelings in her; in his conversation with Cleopas and another disciple on their journey to Emmaus on the day of the resurrection Jesus speaks to them in such a way that they say after he has disappeared from their midst "Did not our hearts burn within us while he talked to us on the road?" (Lk 24:32). The New Testament reveals the risen Jesus as someone who speaks with great intimacy and feeling to those to whom he reveals himself and who evokes strong feelings of love, enthusiasm, faith, joy, peace.

But, some object, are not feelings something that only properly belong to what Paul calls the "physical body," to the "image of the man of dust" and not to the "spiritual body," to the "image of the man of heaven" (1 Cor 15:42–50). Does not Paul say that "flesh and blood cannot inherit the kingdom of God, nor does the perishable inherit the imperishable" (1 Cor 15:50)? As I already indicated, there are feelings that are mere physiological sensations and there are feelings of the heart, such as love, joy, peace. It is feelings of this latter type that the risen Jesus manifests and communicates to those to whom he reveals himself after the resurrection. Of course, just as the risen body is radically transformed in the resurrection, so there is a corresponding transformation and glorification of the human psyche and its capacity for feelings. This means, I suggest, that Jesus' feelings in glory possess a quality and excellence far beyond anything we can presently imagine. Indeed, the most profound human feelings we now experience are but glimmers of the feelings Jesus now experiences in glory and that we too shall experience when Jesus will change our bodies "to be like his glorious body, by the power which enables him even to subject all things to himself" (Phil 3:21).

Projections and Jesus as He Really Is

There is a further question about the feelings of the glorified Jesus. Does he have the feelings toward us that a brother has for a sister or brother, a friend for a friend, the lover for the beloved? Here it is important to stress that the risen Jesus is more, not less, than any human word or title can reveal. This applies to the feelings of the glorified Jesus as well as to all the other dimensions of his transfigured humanity.

The holy women and men of God, the saints in their encounters with Jesus in prayer, have experienced him as loving them in diverse deeply affective ways. Some have experienced Jesus as a deeply caring, intimate friend; others have encountered Jesus as a profoundly compassionate teacher instructing his beloved disciple; others have felt Jesus' presence as that of an older brother affectionately looking after a younger sibling; still others have experienced Jesus as embracing them with the ardor of a bridegroom for his bride. What are we to say of these experiences of the saints of God? Are these experiences purely subjective? Are they projections onto the risen Jesus of feelings that are in no way present in the consciousness of the glorified Jesus?

The experience of the first Christians as expressed in the New Testament provides grounds in varying degrees for ascribing to Jesus the feelings of a brother, teacher, friend, toward the believer. In like manner, the liturgical prayers of the church in its various feasts reflect a belief in Jesus as one who loves his people with the special affections of a brother, teacher, friend, and in other ways as well. This does not mean, of course, that the risen Jesus experiences these feelings in his glorified humanity in exactly the same way as we experience them. But this qualification is not meant to diminish the reality or uniqueness of these feelings. On the contrary, it implies that these feelings exist in the glorified psyche and heart of Jesus in a much richer, more tender, more unique fashion than our heart can even imagine in its most wonderful dreams.

Jesus is then always more, not less, than any mere human words or names can reveal. This means that although the projection of feelings onto the risen Christ is perhaps always at work in our prayer, this projecting is not of necessity so much invalid as it is inadequate. Thus, for example, our projection of feelings of brotherly love onto Jesus more often falls short of, rather than distorts, the reality of Jesus' actual feelings toward us. Most certainly, Jesus in glory experiences himself as brother to every human being. But he experiences himself as brother in a richer, deeper, more profound way than any brother in his earthly life experiences himself as brother to his sisters and brothers in the flesh. And the same is true of all the other human ways of feeling we attribute to the risen Jesus.

Professors Daniel Hardy and David Ford write that "if our conception of God as supremely creative, abundant, generous and free is at all correct, then knowing him is likely continually to stretch our imagination. . . . Far from shunning projection we will exhaust our projective abilities in trying to do justice to God."[17] I think this same insight is valid regarding our intuitive attempts to suggest the richness in affectivity of the glorified human consciousness of Jesus. In our most insightful imaginings we still fall far short of the reality we seek to comprehend. As the author of the epistle to the Ephesians reminds us in the most rhapsodic language, the love of Jesus Christ "surpasses knowledge" (3:19) in its "unsearchable riches" (3:8) and this is no doubt true of all the affections of his glorified human heart.

Prayerful Remembering and Creative Discovering

This "telling of the ways" in which Jesus relates in the depths of his heart and feelings toward each person tends spontaneously to evoke in the follower of Jesus a prayerfully reflective "counting of the ways" in which he or she loves Jesus. Each person who has loved Jesus for some time has a basis in experience for recalling the history of that love. It forms an intimate dimension of the person's autobiography. It is an illuminating experience to retrace the stages in one's love-relationship with Jesus. This process of remembering leads to a sense of gratitude in the follower of Jesus for the graced ways in which he or she has encountered and responded to Jesus in the past. It also awakens in the heart of the believer a desire to be open and responsive to yet other ways in which Jesus reveals himself.

The process of prayerful remembering becomes transformed into a process of creative discovery. What has not been, can be. "How might I love him? Let me count the ways." "Creative discovering" recognizes that love of its very nature inspires a return of love and that specific types of love invite special responses. If, for example, the follower of Jesus discerns that Jesus reveals himself in scripture as a friend, then he or she can prayerfully ask in the presence of Jesus: Do I respond to you in love as a friend to a friend? If the disciple of Jesus finds that she or he responds to him as a learner to a teacher, but not as a friend to a friend, then he or she can ask further: Do I feel an inner prompting to discover you in my heart as a friend as well as a teacher? If I do not presently feel such an interior urging, am I open to such a blossoming of loving desire in the future? Because I have not previously affectively interacted with Jesus as a friend responds to a friend, this does not mean that such an exchange cannot occur in the future. I suggested, for example, to a person well advanced in the spiritual life, that she prayerfully reflect on her very positive experience of her older brother's love for her as a way of getting some affective hint of what Jesus' brotherly love for her might be. This person could scarcely contain her joy when she later told me how she had indeed affectively discovered Jesus as brother in reflecting on her own brother's love and how this discovery had profoundly enriched her prayer relationship with Jesus.

In preparing the present book I sought to encounter Jesus in prayer as friend, beloved, brother, liberator, savior, teacher, healer, Lord and in a variety of other ways as well. I decided that I would only write about those images of Jesus which deeply affected me in my own praying and relating to him from the heart.

In the case of certain images of Jesus, e.g. the image of Jesus as judge, I found that I needed a certain inner healing in order to be able to respond to the image of Jesus as judge in at least a minimally satisfactory fashion. With the aid of the Holy Spirit, I had to reach a point where I could image Jesus as a compassionate judge, a merciful judge. I needed to see this image in the light of other, more spontaneously attractive images of Jesus. On the other hand, although my first encounter with the image of Jesus as "mother" in the writings of the mystic Julian of Norwich at first perplexed me, I grew to appreciate this image as one that especially communicates the care, the tenderness of Jesus. When Jesus uses the metaphor of the "hen" gathering her chicks under her wings (Mt 23:37) to depict his compassionate love of the people of Jerusalem, I find that the symbol evokes deep feelings of trusting love toward Jesus in me.

I must remark at once that my exclusion of a certain image of Jesus from consideration in a chapter of the present book does not imply that I consider the image unimportant or am not affectively attracted by it. For example, I am profoundly moved in mind and heart by the image of Jesus as Lord. But a variety of constraints prevented me from developing a chapter on that image. It is my hope that readers will imitate me in my approach to the discovery and cultivation of images of Jesus and that they will in this way make up for my failure to reflect on certain important images in the present book.

Constantly, in the following chapters, I also reflect not only on the scriptural portraits of Jesus as friend, brother, etc., but also on the concrete examples of saints in their relationships with Jesus and with one another. Certainly, Jesus is the primary example of the perfect friend, liberator, healer. But, Paul exhorted his followers to imitate him as he imitated Christ (1 Cor 11:1). Each of God's saints also provides models for imitation, though the saints had their flaws and must not be imitated uncritically. In any case, Jesus draws us into friendship with him and in this way teaches us how to love not only him but others as friends. Likewise, the saints teach us how to love Jesus as friend and how to love others as friends in a Christly way. We thus learn how to love as friends by letting ourselves be loved by Jesus as friend and by learning to love others with Jesus' own love of friendship. The same kind of transformation occurs as a result of our contemplation of Jesus and his imitators, the saints, in their roles as healers, liberators, lovers, spouses.

Today many excellent critical studies of the lives of the saints are appearing. I have not always had access to the most recent studies and so I recommend that the reader check my own examples in the light of the most recent critical studies of the lives of the saints available.

Imaging Jesus Through Spirit-Feasting and Ignatian Contemplation

There is the practical question about how a person can best come to an appreciative, affective recognition of and response to Jesus as friend, beloved, liberator, savior, healer, teacher, brother, spouse, Lord and God. In my book *Christotherapy II* I outline the stages of what I call the process of appreciative discerning or spirit-feasting.[18] A person can utilize the prayerful process of spirit-feasting as a way of coming to recognize and respond affectively to Jesus in terms of the images by which he reveals himself.

The first step of the spirit-feasting process in the present context is to take a scriptural passage or some incident from the lives of the saints where Jesus is portrayed, for example, as a friend. Next, one should pray for the grace of an appreciative recognition of Jesus as friend and for feelings of friendship toward Jesus. The one praying should then contemplate Jesus in scenes where he shows friendship and invites persons to respond to him in friendship. Hopefully, the one praying will experience some movements of friendly affection toward Jesus and some appreciative recognition of him as loving friend. The final stage in the spirit-feasting process is an ongoing repose and delighting in Jesus as friend and a recalling at various times in the hours and days that follow of the reality of Jesus as friend. Most importantly, the genuineness of the believer's affective growth in friendship with Jesus is actively demonstrated through deeds of love and acts of friendship toward others.

What I propose here is quite similar to the method of contemplation which Saint Ignatius of Loyola outlines in his *Spiritual Exercises*. Ignatius suggests that in contemplating Jesus a person should first place herself or himself in the presence of God; next, the one praying should recall a certain incident in the life of Jesus and engage in a mental, imaginative representation of the concrete circumstances in which Jesus found himself, etc.; then, the contemplator should ask for the grace of certain affective responses to the mystery of Jesus' life that is the subject of the contemplation, e.g. sorrow with Jesus in his suffering, intense joy with Jesus in his resurrection, etc. Finally, Ignatius emphasizes that love proves itself in deeds and that the one who prays should ask herself or himself: " 'What have I done for Christ?' 'What am I doing for Christ?' What ought I to do for Christ.' "[19]

Certain cautions are worth noting concerning the methods of praying I just outlined. First, the Holy Spirit is the primary agent in these prayer processes, and the one praying must listen to the Spirit in quiet attentiveness and not seek to dominate the prayer process. Second, if the Holy Spirit grants an appreciative recognition, for example, of Jesus as friend and a heartfelt response to him of friendly affection, the one praying should accept the gift with gratitude. But if "nothing" seems to happen in prayer, the contemplator should bless God, in any case, and acknowledge that quiet growth is taking place, even though the one praying may not recognize it. Third, Jesus reveals himself to individuals in ways especially appropriate to their present needs and most often in harmony with their psychic temperament. This means that the one praying should contemplate Jesus now as friend, now as brother, etc. in order to discover how Jesus intends to speak to him or her and what kind of response he asks. Fourth, there are times when individuals are called into an inner quiet, a simple, silent abiding in God's presence. It is most helpful to have a spiritual guide who can aid one in discerning how it is best to pray at a given time and stage in one's spiritual development.

"Centering Prayer" and Contemplative Imaging of Jesus

Today such excellent spiritual writers as the Trappist monk Fr. M. Basil Pennington[20] and Cistercian monk Fr. Thomas Keating[21] have retrieved and refined the ancient Christian practice of "centering prayer." In this form of prayer the emphasis is on letting go of thoughts, imaginings, sensible affections and centering on God dwelling within us. Both Fr. Pennington and Fr. Keating suggest that the contemplators should place themselves in God's presence and then repeat inwardly a sacred word, e.g. "Jesus," until they find themselves at the "center," quietly abiding in God's presence. When distractions arise those praying should repeat the sacred word and then let go of it again as inner silence returns.

I do not think that there is any conflict between my stress in this book on the prayerful contemplation of Jesus as friend, brother, beloved and the emphasis on centering prayer of various spiritual writers. Different forms of prayer are useful for persons at various stages of spiritual development. There are also times in every person's life for thoughtful, prayerful reflections as well as for simple, quiet periods of adoration. It is likewise true that a more active contemplation of Jesus, e.g. imaging him in friendly exchanges with Mary and Martha, can gradually evolve into a peaceful abiding in the presence of Jesus the friend, without the occurrence of active imagining. This kind of shift often occurs in persons who habitually recite the rosary.

Further, the practice of centering prayer in no way stands in opposition to a focus on Jesus in his humanity or in his divinity. Fr. Pennington recommends that the practitioner of centering prayer "daily meet the Word in a deeply personal way and let him speak to mind and heart through the life-giving words of his revelation"[22] and engage in "the other forms of prayer: the celebration of the sacraments and the Eucharist and communing with the Lord in Holy Scripture."[23] Indeed, Fr. Keating asks the question: "What, then, is our principal focus in centering prayer?" and he responds: "It is to deepen our relationship with Jesus Christ, the Divine-Human Being."[24]

The Role of Consolation in Active and Contemplative Vocations

We must note also how the prayer experiences of persons can differ significantly in accordance with their particular vocations and life-situation. Jesuit Fr. Thomas Clancy, for example, in an article entitled "Feeling Bad about Feeling Good," makes the point that Jesuits, who generally lead quite active, apostolic lives, generally have a need for joy, peace, love and various spiritual consolations in their prayer and daily living in order most effectively to live out their particular callings. He writes with some humor:

> Apostolic religious orders which have a certain dynamism tend to attract people whose lives lack that placid serenity, that unchangeable peace that characterizes some of the older orders, notably the Benedictines. I have lived for thirty-six years in the Society, and I would not consider balance and Benedictine *pax* to be the salient traits of the greatest Jesuits I have known. Most of them are either way up (generally), or way down (from time to time). Joy and consolation characterized their lives, but it was not always there.[25]

I must add that Fr. Clancy wrote his article because he had of late found too much sadness among his Jesuit brothers. I should likewise emphasize that the consolations Clancy speaks of are not so much superficial sensible consolations, but rather the consolations of deep faith, eager hope, delighting love. Clancy, of course, in accord with the advice of Saint Ignatius, points out that the Jesuit cannot unconditionally demand consolations from God and must exercise patience, creative, prayerful discerning, and active submission to God's will when consolations are absent.

Interestingly, Fr. Thomas Keating remarks that the individuals he has dealt with who have the most "exuberant" mystical lives are either married or in an active ministry. Keating observes that less than five percent of the cloistered contemplatives he has known have the type of mystical experiences that John of the Cross or Teresa of Avila speak of. Instead the "consolations" of most cloistered contemplatives "are few and far between." Keating surmises that "those who are in the world doubtless need more help in order to survive" and that "perhaps God does not help cloistered folks in the same way because he has decided that they have enough support from the structures of their enclosed lifestyle."[26] Keating's observations lend support to Clancy's argument concerning the need of apostolically involved Jesuits for consolations.

My primary motivating force in writing this book is the inner experience of the consoling, inspiring, life-giving love of Jesus Christ. The love of Christ "impels" (2 Cor 5:14) me to seek to share my joy in his love with others. Jesuit theologian Harvey Egan observes that Saint Ignatius was gifted with a "passionate love for Christ."[27] I believe that it is part of the charism of a follower of Saint Ignatius to fall deeply in love with Jesus Christ. "Ignatius' mystical experiences moved easily from Jesus in his humanity to Jesus as Son, the second person in the Trinity. By penetrating to Christ's very heart, he mystically grasped in and through Christ's humanity that Jesus was totally his God."[28]

In my books *Christotherapy*[29] and *Christotherapy II* my love for Jesus and the experience of his healing touch led me to focus in a special way on Jesus as healer. Egan, however, brilliantly observes that Ignatius' "unusual mystical experiences integrated him" and that "his mysticism is one of integration and personal wholeness."[30] I cannot lay claim myself to anything like the gift of complete personal wholeness, but I have found that the love of Jesus continues to draw me toward the goal of deeper integration. This inner experience leads me to focus in the present book not only on Jesus as healer, but also as giver of gifts of high level integration of mind, psyche, heart and spirit. And we have always before us, beckoning us onward, the example of Saint Ignatius in whom Christ effected "a balanced union and harmonious interaction of all his volitional, intellectual, psychological, and emotional powers."[31]

Loving Jesus as "Christointegration"

Most certainly loving Jesus Christ is supremely worthwhile in itself because, as we read in the gospel of John, "this is eternal life, that they know thee the only true God, and Jesus Christ whom thou hast sent" (Jn 17:3). But, as I just indicated, loving Jesus Christ is also a dynamic, graced process with many transformative effects. The word "integration" sums up well the process. The fusion of the name "Christ" with the term "integration" is an appropriate wedding of words because the mission of Christ is to integrate. Jesus' goal is to bring wholeness to the divided human heart, to unify human beings split from one another and from God, to re-establish harmony among all things in heaven and on earth (Col 1:20).

Saint Augustine somewhere wrote: "Love God and do what you will." Without injury to Augustine's basic insight we might say with equal boldness: "Love Jesus Christ and do what you will." This might seem like the granting of a license for any kind of behavior. But the opposite is the case. Augustine understood that the more perfect a person's love of God is, the more the individual will love whatever God loves, value whatever God values, and do whatever is in harmony with divine love. The same may be said regarding a person's love of Jesus Christ. The deeper and richer the individual's love of Jesus is, the more he or she will love what Jesus loves, value what he values and act in the way he acts.

The love of Jesus becomes the measure of all else. This love tends to set up an order among all other loves, desires. There is an ongoing movement toward a harmonizing of desires and an integration of the person on all levels of thinking, desiring, acting. The follower of Jesus comes to say: "It is no longer I who think, I who love, I who act, but Christ who thinks, loves, acts in me." This startling transformation is possible because it is the very nature of love to effect an ever more total union of heart and mind between the lover and the beloved. Here the process of Christointegration unfolds at an ever deepening level. There is an ongoing healing of the self divided against itself and an ever deepening unity of the self with Jesus. At the same time the person in love with Jesus displays more spontaneity in living and acting than ever before; and, Augustine's paradoxical precept, "Love God and do what you will," is visibly lived out for all to see.

Loving Jesus Christ not only heals and integrates the divided self, it also heals ruptures in interpersonal relationships and integrates the self with others. The follower of Jesus is inwardly drawn to love not only Jesus, but also all those whom Jesus loves. The lover of Jesus is also interiorly inspired to love those whom Jesus loves *as* Jesus loves them. The follower of Jesus Christ is gradually transformed into the one he or she loves, into "another Christ," and loves more and more with the characteristics of Jesus' own love.

But Jesus Christ is concretely "all things to all." This means, for example, that in the process of loving Jesus Christ as friend the lover becomes gradually transformed into Christ as friend. The lover can say: "Christ the friend lives in me." The lover of Jesus is inwardly drawn to love all those whom Christ calls friends and to love them *as* Christ loves his friends. The lover of Jesus *as* friend is transformed into a Christly friend or, more simply, a "Christ-friend." Secular language refers to a "soul-mate." The soul-mate is a person compatible with another in point of view, attitude, disposition, sensitivity. A "Christ-friend" is one who loves Christ as a friend, possesses the mind and heart of Christ and loves the friends of Jesus with Christ's own love of friendship. Because Jesus Christ is concretely "all things to all" the same transformation

occurs when a person loves Jesus Christ as teacher, healer, liberator, and in other ways as well. The loving disciple of Jesus Christ is
transformed little by little into a "Christ-teacher," a "Christ-
healer," a "Christ-liberator."

Loving Jesus Christ is, indeed, a transforming mystery that is
appropriately named "Christointegration." The fruits of love of
Jesus are wholeness, inner integrity, communion with others.
Loving Jesus Christ also opens us up to an embrace of the cosmos,
for the author of the epistle to the Colossians reminds us that in
Christ "all things were created, in heaven and on earth, visible and
invisible . . . all things were created through him and for him"
(Col 1:16). And Paul in Romans tell us that the whole of creation is
in bondage and waits with "eager longing for the revealing of the
sons of God . . . because creation itself will be set free from its
bondage to decay" (Rom 8:19–21). Christianity teaches the
goodness and reality of matter; it espouses a view of the intimate
relationship between humankind and the whole cosmos. Today
the lesson is clear that human beings need to care for the earth, if
they themselves are to survive and thrive. If we are to love our
bodies properly we need to love air, earth, fire and water and all
the elements that sustain us. We are called to live in harmony with
nature, to utilize its resources without abusing them. The earth is
our "greater body," and integration with it is part of our calling in
Christ, since the world itself is created "through him and for him."

This book is at its deepest level not so much a call to the imitation of Christ as it is an invitation to celebrate and grow in the love
of Christ. The imitation of Christ naturally flows out of the transforming mystery of loving Jesus Christ. The hope is that prayerful
contemplation of Jesus as brother, savior, healer, liberator, friend,
beloved, spouse will draw the readers to new encounters with
Jesus Christ and a deepening in the intensity of their love for him
and for all those whom he loves.

Clearly, a book on loving Jesus Christ does not pretend to exhaust the possibilities of reflections on our love-encounters with
God. Our God is a Trinity of persons, and eternal life consists in
loving, praising and glorifying the Father, the Son and the Holy
Spirit. Certainly books on the transforming love of the Father and
the Spirit are equally needed today. But each author must follow
the particular inspirations for writing that he or she is given at a
particular time. Also, no one can write adequately about Jesus
Christ without reference to the Holy Spirit and the Father. For it

is the Holy Spirit who leads us into an ever richer comprehension of the unsearchable riches of Jesus Christ and it is, above all, through Jesus that the Father reveals himself.

Harvey Egan observes that "Ignatius penetrated to the very heart of innertrinitarian life" and "experienced each of the three divine persons, [and] their mutual indwelling." At the same time Egan notes that "Ignatius experienced how the Son is present essentially in the Father" and that even Ignatius' "Father-centered mysticism contains a Son-directed aspect because the Father, for Ignatius, is the *Father of such a Son.*"[32] I have constantly found in my own prayer life that the deeper I grow in my love for Jesus Christ, the more my love for the Father and the Holy Spirit grows. The ultimate fruit of the process of Christointegration is then an ever deeper entering into the inner love-life of the Trinity itself. This goal is beautifully expressed in Jesus' prayer to the Father "that they may be one even as we are one, I in them and thou in me, that they may be perfectly one" (Jn 17:22–23).

On a very practical note, one way to engage profitably in the reading of the following chapters is to keep some of the following questions in mind. How, for example, did I first come to know of Jesus? Are my memories of Jesus, as I first encountered him, positive or negative? Have I grown in my understanding and love of Jesus or has my relationship with Christ been static? Is there one image of Christ that is dominant in my consciousness? If so, has this image always been dominant or have other images captivated me at earlier stages of my development? Have I consciously turned to Jesus in times of acute suffering or great joy? Who are the people who have mainly mediated Christ to me? Have attitudes toward these people perhaps affected at a deep level the way I affectively view Jesus Christ? To what extent has my sexuality, my temperament influenced my relationship with Jesus? Am I enthusiastic about the possibility of discovering new dimensions of the mystery of Jesus Christ? If I am not excited by new possibilities in relating to Jesus, why is this so? Is there anything I can do about my lack of enthusiasm? What might be blocking me? Am I at least willing to expose myself to something new? Do I believe that what has not yet been, can be?

Finally, I recommend that the reader begin with the chapter on the image of Jesus that most spontaneously attracts him or her. It is better initially to move toward what attracts than toward what puzzles, repels or leaves one affectively indifferent. The contemplator may then little by little be surprised by new revelations, ever more joyous disclosures by the Holy Spirit of the inexhaustibly rich mystery of Jesus Christ.

Notes

1. Cf. Albert Nolan, *Jesus Before Christianity* (New York: Orbis Press, 1978), pp. 57–58; Gerard S. Sloyan, *Jesus in Focus* (Mystic, Connecticut: Twenty-Third Publications, 1983), pp. 129–136.

2. Cf. Elisabeth Schüssler Fiorenza, *In Memory of Her* (New York: Crossroad Publishing Company, 1984), pp. 118–159; Sandra M. Schneiders, *Women and the Word* (New York: Paulist Press, 1986).

3. This is not to deny that the community dimension is also present in John's gospel.

4. See Raymond Brown, *The Churches the Apostles Left Behind* (New York: Paulist Press, 1984), pp. 84–85.

5. See John Wijngaards, *Experiencing Jesus* (Notre Dame, Indiana: Ave Maria Press,) 1981, esp. pp. 16–18.

6. Teresa of Avila, *Interior Castle*, translated and edited by E. Allison Peers, (New York: Doubleday, Image Book, 1961).

7. Ibid., pp. 177–178.

8. Ibid., p. 185.

9. Karl Rahner, *Foundations of Christian Faith*, trans. by William Dych (New York: Seabury Press, 1978), pp. 308–309.

10. Antonio T. de Nicolas, *Powers of Imagining, Ignatius de Loyola: A Philosophical Hermeneutic of Imagining Through the Collected Works of Ignatius of Loyola with a Translation of these Works* (Albany: State University of New York Press, 1986), No. 77 of the *Spiritual Diary*, p. 203.

11. Ibid., No. 73, p. 202.

12. Ibid., No. 75, p. 203.

13. Ann Belford Ulanov, *Picturing God* (New York: Cowley Publications, 1986), p. 164.

14. Urban T. Holmes, *A History of Christian Spirituality* (New York: Seabury Press, 1980), pp. 17–20.

15. Cf. Bernard Lonergan, *Method in Theology* (New York: Herder and Herder, 1972), pp. 31–33.

16. Dietrich von Hildebrand, *The Sacred Heart* (Baltimore: Helicon Press Inc., 1965), pp. 25–73.

17. Daniel Hardy and David Ford, *Praising and Knowing God* (Philadelphia: Westminister Press, 1985), p. 111.

18. Bernard Tyrrell, *Christotherapy II* (New York: Paulist Press, 1982), pp. 126–128.

19. Louis Puhl, *The Spiritual Exercises of St. Ignatius* (Chicago: Loyola University Press, 1951), p. 28.

20. M. Basil Pennington, *Centering Prayer* (New York: Doubleday, 1980).

21. Thomas Keating, *Open Mind, Open Heart* (New York: Amity House, 1986).

22. Pennington, ibid., p. 167.

23. Ibid., p. 188.

24. Keating, ibid., p. 50.

25. Thomas Clancy, "Feeling Bad about Feeling Good," *Studies*, XI, January 1979, No. 1 (St. Louis: American Assistancy Seminar on Jesuit Spirituality, St. Louis University, 1979), p. 25.

26. Ibid., p. 11.

27. Harvey Egan, *Ignatius Loyola the Mystic* (Wilmington: Glazier, 1987), p. 91.

28. Ibid., pp. 93–94.

29. Bernard Tyrrell, *Christotherapy* (New York: Paulist Press, 1986).

30. Egan, ibid., p. 200.

31. Ibid.

32. Ibid., p. 93.

2

Savior and
Healer of Hearts

A grandfather, not long before his death, sent a card with a printed prayer on it to his twenty year old grandson. On the back of the card he wrote in somewhat faltering hand: "Always depend upon Jesus and he will carry you through, for he is most willing to do; he is most willing to do it; he is most willing to do." I cherish the card to this day. Karl Rahner, just two or three years before his death at the age of eighty, told a story about a conversation he had with a theologian who in his theories about Jesus seemed to have little to do with the Jesus of normal Christian faith. Rahner said that "at one point I put in with, 'Yes, you see, you're actually only really dealing with Jesus when you throw your arms around him and realize right down to the bottom of your being that this is something you can still do today.' "[1] My grandfather, a farmer, and the premier theologian, Karl Rahner, possessed in common a profound, yet very simple and tender, trusting love of Jesus.

One New Testament title for Jesus that from age to age has evoked a deeply felt loving response to him is the name "savior." The words "healer" and "liberator" are closely related in meaning to the name "savior." The New Testament does not use the nouns "healer" and "liberator" to name Jesus, but it does describe Jesus as healing various diseases (Mt 19:2) and as seeking to free people from unjust burdens (Lk 11:46). Clearly the biblical understanding of Jesus' saving action includes within its scope his healing and liberating deeds. But the very richness of Jesus' saving action justifies introducing such titles as "healer" and "liberator" as a means of highlighting different dimensions of Jesus' saving work.

Personal History in Imaging Jesus

The image of Jesus as savior, of course, dominates the history of Christianity far more than the images of Jesus as healer or as liberator. But for a growing number of Christians in the present age the images of Jesus as healer or liberator exercise a powerful attraction and evoke deep feelings of love, hope, courage. The emphasis on gifts of healing in the charismatic movement and the work of groups inspired by Jean Vanier, Mother Teresa and others with the mentally handicapped, the abandoned sick and dying have focused the attention of Christians once again on Jesus the healer. The civil rights movement in the United States, the ongoing quest for justice for the exploited and enslaved throughout the world—often at the price of martyrdom—have highlighted the reality of Jesus as liberator.

But the stress on Jesus as healer and liberator need not and should not mean a forgetfulness of Jesus as savior. For the authentic Christian it is never a matter of choosing between Jesus as healer and Jesus as savior or between Jesus as liberator and Jesus as savior. Rather, Jesus is loved and hoped in as the savior who frees human beings from the most radical evil, from sin and eternal death, but who also seeks to bring about healing of illness and freedom from all forms of oppression—as much as possible in the present life and totally in the life to come.

Each Christian has his or her own particular history of responding to various salvational images of Jesus. Some believers respond to Jesus from the heart as savior but not as healer or liberator. Others relate with deep feeling to Jesus as savior and healer but not as liberator, and vice versa. I first affectively responded to Jesus as savior and in more recent years as healer and then liberator. Since no theological logic requires an author to reflect on these three titles in a certain order, it seems best to me to treat them in terms of my own voyage of discovery. This tactic helps assure that my approach will be concrete rather than abstract, experiential rather than merely arbitrary. Also, since I have written at length about Jesus as healer in two previous books,[2] I will include my more recent reflections on Jesus as healer in the present chapter, and dedicate a separate chapter to the consideration of Jesus as liberator.

Christmas Festivity and the Child-Savior

In my case, as perhaps for many brought up from infancy as Christians, the first memories of Jesus as "savior" are permeated with the bright, warm, joyous images of Christmas. My Christmas remembrances form a constellation of joyful elements: the crib with the infant Jesus, Mary, Joseph, the shepherds, the bright star, the kings; the singing of Christmas carols; the gathering of grand-parents, aunts, uncles, cousins; the exchange of gifts, eating and drinking together; deep personal warmth among family members. The songs and scriptural readings of the Christmas season con-stantly repeat the word "savior" and apply it to Jesus. "To us a child is born, to us a son is given" (Is 9:6). "To you is born this day . . . a Savior, who is Christ the Lord. . . . You will find a babe wrapped in swaddling clothes and lying in a manger" (Lk 2:11–12). For me then, as a young child, "salvation" meant a wonderful gift from God to me and those I loved in the form of a baby. Somehow this baby loved me and I could love him and trust in him. And he brought all those I loved together. Christmas was the happiest time of the year and Jesus, the "savior," was the center and cause of all this joy and gladness.

Some striking similarities exist between the way Jesus was first presented to me as a child and my initial feeling responses to him, and the manner in which Jesus revealed himself to his first disci-ples and their heartfelt responses to him. Clearly, there are also important differences, since in the first instance we are dealing with the encounter of a young child with Jesus as presented to him, especially through the celebration of a feast recalling the birth of Jesus; in the latter case, we are reflecting on the historical Jesus in his initial dealings with those called to be his disciples. Yet there is perhaps a special legitimacy in my comparison in the sense that Jesus showed a special tenderness toward little children and said "let the children come to me, do not hinder them; for to such belongs the kingdom of God" (Mk 10:14). It is this same Jesus, whose birthday is celebrated every Christmas with such joy by children, who as an adult expressed annoyance when his disciples tried to keep the children from touching him and as Mark tells us "took [the children] in his arms and blessed them, laying his hands upon them" (Mk 10:16).

God's Eternal Youth and "Children with White Beards"

Karl Rahner tells us that at Christmas we celebrate the birth of a child "in whom the eternal youth of God breaks in upon this world definitively and victoriously."[3] Certainly, the infant Jesus attracts children because of his freshness, his availability, his vulnerability as a newborn child. He evokes in children feelings of wonder, delight, affection. Jesus in his public ministry likewise reveals "the eternal youth of God" in his tender relationship with his beloved "abba," (Rom 8:15; Mk 14:36) in the enthusiasm of his preaching of the "good news" and in his joy in God's revelation of his "secrets" to little ones (Mt 11:25). Jesus spontaneously attracted little children to him. He also inspired wonder at his graciousness and new message in those adults who possessed receptive, childlike hearts. It is these latter whom Catherine de Hueck Doherty describes as " 'children' with white beards and white hair."[4]

The celebration of Christmas and Jesus' inauguration of his public life are both interpersonal events of a joyous nature with a unique gift of God at their center. At Christmas we commemorate God's coming among us in the form of a child. The infant Jesus is "Emmanuel," which means "God with us" (Mt 1:23). My spontaneous response to this Christmas gift as a child was joy. Jesus began his public life by announcing "good news," the wonderful tidings that salvation was at hand: "For behold, the kingdom of God is in the midst of you" (Lk 17:21). Jesus "concentrated all the varied expectations of salvation into a single theme, participation in the kingdom of God."[5] Jesus taught that in the gift of the kingdom a new intimacy with God and with one another was at hand. Jesus compared the reception of this gift to the discovery of a treasure hidden in a field. The basic feeling response of the one discovering the treasure is great joy (Mt 13:44). God's graciousness and loving kindness are at the core of Christmas and of Jesus' proclamation of the presence of the kingdom among us, and the spontaneous response of the human heart is gratitude, joy.

An air of festivity belongs to Christmas and Jesus' initial preaching of the coming of the reign of the "abba" among us. Believers celebrate together at Christmas; they eat and drink with one another and rejoice in their companionship and common sharing in the friendship of God. Jesus began his public ministry by comparing the coming of the kingdom among us to a festive participation in a wedding party. Jesus did not conduct his ministry in the ascetic mode of John the Baptist. Rather, he came "eating and drinking" (Mt 11:19). Jesus' playful, gracious words to Zacchaeus, a chief tax collector, who had climbed a tree to get a look at the rabbi from Nazareth, typify his way of announcing the "good news." "And when Jesus came to the place he looked up and said to him, 'Zacchaeus, make haste and come down; for I must stay at your house today' " (Lk 19:5). Luke tells us that Zacchaeus "made haste and came down, and received him joyfully" (19:6). There is an aura of delight, of festive celebration that characterizes the "springtime" of Jesus' public ministry, though the dark element of rejection also appears early on.

Joyous News for the Poor

Luke in describing the birth of Jesus recounts that the first persons invited by God's angels to visit the newborn child are shepherds, tending their flocks in nearby fields. Matthew in his account of the birth of Jesus tells us that wise men, guided by a star, came from the east to worship the child Jesus and offer him gifts. The nativity scenes in churches and homes show to children the newly born Jesus surrounded by poor folk, by his humble parents and finally by three wise men with gifts. The sense the child has is that Jesus is for everyone. And the response is one of wonder, delight, trust, affection. Likewise, the child learns that receiving gifts calls for the response of giving gifts. Generosity leads to generosity. And God's invitation to the poor shepherds to be the first ones to encounter the infant Jesus is reenacted by Jesus who at the beginning of his public ministry invites all, but, in a special way, the poor and despised, to enter into the kingdom of the "abba." When John the Baptist in prison inquires of Jesus through his disciples if he is "the one who is to come," Jesus replies: "Go and tell John what you hear and see: the blind receive their sight and the lame walk, lepers are cleansed . . . and the poor have good news preached to them" (Mt 11:3–5).

Jesus shares the news of the kingdom with the poor and the least respected members of his society. And he invites the prostitutes and sinners to table-community with him. As we just saw, for example, he summons Zacchaeus, a tax collector, to dine with him and share in the good news of the kingdom. Jesus' spontaneous sharing of himself and the good news with the poor and contemned of society led his enemies to describe him as a "glutton and a drunkard, a friend of tax collectors and sinners" (Mt 11:19). When they saw how Jesus dealt with Zacchaeus they murmured: "He has gone in to be the guest of a man who is a sinner" (Lk 19:7). But Jesus' offer of table-sharing evoked in those who accepted his invitation deeply felt joy, gratitude, affection. Luke tells us that Zacchaeus in his joy at Jesus' gracious kindness toward him promised to give half of his goods to the poor and to give four times as much as he had stolen to anyone he might have defrauded (19:8). Jesus comes to us bearing the good news that God loves us, despite our poverty, our wretchedness, our sinfulness. The gift of unmerited divine love is the core of the Christmas message and of the preaching of Jesus.

Adolescence and Guilt

In the course of my Catholic grade school and high school education, I was taught about the sin of the first parents of our race and how Jesus died for our sins to restore us to the friendship with God, which Adam and Eve had lost. To the joyous image of Jesus as savior in the crib at Bethlehem, there was added the sorrowful image of Jesus as savior through his suffering and death on the cross. I was taught that through the reception of the sacrament of baptism I was restored to friendship with God, to the "state of grace." But I was also instructed that if I committed a serious sin, I would "fall out of" the "state of grace" and be in danger of damnation, unless I confessed my sins and did penance. To my early childhood feelings of joy, trust, tenderness in the presence of the infant Jesus were added feelings of shame, guilt and fear at the thought of my own sins and their possible consequences.

Certainly, Jesus made the good news of God's gift of forgiveness the center of his message, but he also called his listeners to repentance for their sins. "The time is fulfilled, and the kingdom of God is at hand; repent, and believe in the gospel" (Mk 1:15). Jesus perceived human sinfulness as a basic reality and he called individuals to a recognition of their condition and a radical change of heart. Nor is there any less a need for conversion of mind and heart today.

The Reign of God: Blessing or Burden?

Jean Vanier, who has spent so many years of his life living with and loving mentally handicapped individuals, states: "Christian doctrine on the wounded heart, or original sin, appears to me the one reality which is easily verified."[6] Vanier says that "it would be an error to believe that if there were no oppressive parents, if there was no oppressive society, then we would have only beautiful children, loving, happy, integrated within themselves."[7] Rather, Vanier believes that "in the heart of each of us, there is division, there is fear, there is fragility; there is a defense system which protects our vulnerability, there is flight from pain, there is evil and there is darkness."[8] It is then necessary for individuals to acknowledge their sinfulness and to accept Jesus' offer of forgiveness. But things go awry when the sinner focuses more on his or her sinfulness than on Jesus' gift of forgiveness. Fear and guilt can dominate the consciousness of the sinner instead of trust in Jesus. But Jesus wants life, not death, and his religion is not, "first of all, a series of laws which one must obey,"[9] but "a religion of mercy."[10]

It is important for each of us to ask ourselves whether we basically view Jesus' message to us as a blessing or a burden, as a consolation or a threat of condemnation. For the way we view Jesus' role in our own lives will determine the manner we communicate Jesus to others. Here again our feelings are extremely important. Is my basic affective stance toward Jesus one of fear or of trust, despair or hope, sadness or joy?

Carl Jung and "Lord Jesus"

Unfortunately, some persons, often through no fault of their own, develop a deeply felt negative image of Jesus early on and find themselves blocked in their ability to trust in him and his offer of salvation and forgiveness. Carl Jung, for example, in his autobiography recounts that very early he came to associate "Lord Jesus" with death, with solemn men dressed in black, with women weeping. "Certain persons who had been around previously would no longer be there. Then I would hear that they had been buried, and that Lord Jesus had taken them to himself."[11] Jung also heard his father speak of Jesuit priests in a fearful way and he connected the word "Jesuit" with the name Jesus he had learned in a prayer. These experiences, together with a dream that preoccupied Jung all his life,[12] left him basically unable to relate to "Lord Jesus" in a positive way. Jung felt a certain distrust toward "Lord Jesus" and was not able to overcome it. He writes: "In later years . . . I made every effort to force myself to take the required positive attitude toward Christ. But I could never succeed in overcoming my secret distrust."[13] Jung began his autobiographical reflections in 1957 and died in 1961. To the end he was unable to overcome his basic distrust of Jesus.

Damien of Molokai

In a situation quite the opposite of Jung's are those individuals who develop a basically positive trust in Jesus that remains with them throughout their lives, though at times they have to struggle with a strong sense of sinfulness. Father Damien de Veuster, for example, "the apostle of the lepers" of Molokai, was a person who seems to have grown up with a very positive image of Jesus and trust in him. As a young man Damien joined a religious institute which had as a major charism devotion to Jesus and adoration of him present in the Blessed Sacrament. One of Damien's biographers mentions that "he had an especially tender devotion to our Lord Jesus Christ."[14] Before Damien began his four and one half month journey by sea from Europe to Hawaii, where he would remain until he died, he wrote with great enthusiasm: "It is Jesus Christ who preserves His missionaries from all dangers, who commands the winds to be still. . . . It is He who will make us enjoy unsuspected happiness in the midst of tribulations, sufferings, contradictions."[15] And later in the midst of his work for the lepers of Molokai he wrote: "Without the Blessed Sacrament, a position like mine would be unbearable. But having our Lord near me, I am always happy and have the drive to work for the good of my dear lepers."[16]

Damien, unlike Jung, seems to have developed early on a positive image of Jesus, and this positive image remained with him throughout his life. But Damien did at times have to struggle with feelings of guilt and an exaggerated sense of his own sinfulness. He did not have a confessor readily available to him, and this was a great deprivation for him. At one point he became rather obsessed with what he thought might have been an act of disobedience to his superior. In one letter he wrote: "I can only wait patiently for the arrival of a priest. Pray then and get others to pray for me. . . . While waiting for a confessor, I confess from time to time before the Blessed Sacrament."[17] Damien was a saint, and his sense of sinfulness was very likely rooted more in an acute awareness of God's holiness rather than in some real disobedience on his part. And, overall, Father Damien radiated a loving trust in Jesus that had a very powerful, saving impact on those whom he served and for whom he gave his life.

"I Have a Sinne of Feare"

Yet, there exist other individuals—and I speak from a certain personal experience here—who are gifted in their lives with a very positive, affectionate trust in Jesus, but who are assailed at times with such strong mistrust of themselves that their trust in Jesus seems to pass into a kind of eclipse. The trust remains, but it is difficult to discern it. The poet John Donne expresses the tension between mistrust of self and trust in the saving love of Jesus in the poem *A Hymne to God the Father*.[18] In a mounting series of poetic questions Donne asks God if he will forgive his first sin, then a sin into which he falls again and again, then a sin by which he brought others to sin, and a sin "which I did shunne a yeare or two: but wallowed in, a score." In the last stanza of the poem Donne reveals the deepest struggle of his heart:

> I have a sinne of feare, that when I have spunne
>   My last thred, I shall perish on the shore;
> Sweare by thy selfe, that at my death thy sonne
>   Shall shine as he shines now, and heretofore;
> And, having done that, Thou haste done,
>   I feare no more.

In the end Donne lets go of his fear and places full confidence in God and the saving presence of God's Son who he trusts will shine like the sun at his death. There is a courage in Donne's final act of trust in God. Karl Rahner describes such an act of courageous faith when he writes that "if someone, perhaps in apparent total hopelessness and despair, nevertheless hopes that he is hoping (since even hope itself cannot be established for certain as a solid fact on which further calculations could be securely based, but that very hope must be hoped for) . . . then that courageous hope is always realized."[19] I have found that when things look bleak it is helpful to say to God from one's heart: "Lord, I believe that your mercy is greater than my misery!" Here there is a letting go of an unhealthy focus on self and an entrusting of oneself to the divine mercy.

Catherine de Hueck Doherty reminds us that we can also cling to guilt instead of letting go of it: "How often have we gone to confession, been forgiven, but remained uneasy, tragically still feeling guilty of those very sins we have just confessed to God."[20] She wisely remarks that in these instances "we must begin to understand that we must love one another, and that means first forgiving ourselves and everybody else!" In the instance of fear and of guilt we need to remind ourselves that the "gospel" is just that, namely, "good news," and that God is truly "greater than our hearts" (1 Jn 3:20) and more eager to forgive us and more clever about realizing his aims than we can hope or dream.

If all authentic personal love of Jesus is generative, a love that overflows into love for others, then the love of Jesus as savior should manifest itself in a special fruitfulness. But what very concretely are some of the ways in which the personal love of Jesus as savior reveals itself in relation to others?

"Jesus Rejoices That He Is Our Savior"

One of the most basic ways our love of Jesus as savior becomes a fruitful love is through our heartfelt rejoicing in the saving love of Jesus. Julian of Norwich tells us that Jesus rejoices in a most special way "that he is our savior"[21] and wants us to rejoice that he is our savior: "See how I love you" and "see what delight and bliss I have in your salvation, and for my love rejoice with me."[22] Joy is contagious. The happy person attracts others and draws them into rejoicing in the source of the jubilant one's joy. Karl Rahner says that Christians ideally are "those who smile," "those from whom the light of their redemption radiates out."[23] Where the joy that results from the love of Jesus as savior shines forth to others "our witness" becomes "credible" and others can "recognize in us" that we do "indeed proclaim the *euangelion*, the good tidings which sound so different from the talk that goes on in the streets of the world."[24] In effect, the redeemed individual, through his or her very presence, issues an invitation to others to "enter into the joy of the savior" (cf. Mt 25:21).

The Fruitfulness of Apostolic Sufferings

Another way the Christian's love of Jesus as savior becomes generative is through the "use" of suffering for the good of others. Paul in Colossians writes: "Now I rejoice in my sufferings for your sake, and in my flesh I complete what is lacking in Christ's afflictions for the sake of his body, that is, the church" (Col 1:24). I note in passing that scripture scholars dispute the Pauline authorship of Colossians. But, to avoid unnecessary confusion, I will follow the classical authors in referring to Paul as the author of Colossians. Paul, then, frequently met with rejection and persecution as he announced the gospel. But he viewed these apostolic sufferings as a sharing in the lot of Jesus and as a way of benefiting the members of Christ's body, the church. For the Christian the victory of Christ through his death and resurrection is such that any suffering, no matter how meaningless it may appear, can be utilized in a positive way. "We know that in everything God works for good with those who love him" (Rom 8:28). Paul's words about completing through his own suffering "what is lacking in Christ's afflictions for the sake of his body" have constantly provided followers of Jesus the savior with a sense of meaning and fruitfulness in the midst of their sufferings.

The Ongoing Suffering of Jesus in His Followers

Dorothy Day wrote that "the mystery of suffering has a different aspect under the New Covenant, since Christ died on the Cross and took on Himself men's sins."[25] She observed that "St. Paul teaches that we can fill up the sufferings of Christ, that we must share in the sufferings of the world to lessen them, to show our love for our brothers," and that "we can trust with Abraham that for even ten just men" God "will not destroy the city."[26] Dorothy Day understood that in some mysterious way through our sufferings, united to the suffering of Christ, we can share in the saving work of Jesus and help others. Oscar Romero, inspired by the words of Paul, reminded his flock in one of his pastoral letters that the church is the "Body of Christ in history"[27] and that "it is the church's duty to lend its voice to Christ so that he may speak, its feet so that he may walk today's world, its hands to build the kingdom, and to offer all its members 'to make up all that has still to be undergone by Christ' (Col 1:24)."[28] Archbishop Romero, like Paul, carried "in his body the death of Jesus, so that the life of Jesus [might] be manifested in our bodies" (2 Cor 4:10) by offering his life as a martyr of love for the poor.

Mother Teresa, in the spirit of Paul, says that "suffering in itself is nothing, but suffering that shares in the Passion of Christ is a wonderful gift and a sign of love."[29] She tells her sisters that "Jesus wanted to help us by sharing our life, our loneliness, our agony, our death" and that "He permits us to do the same"[30] in the context of the service of our sisters and brothers. She reminds her sisters that "the afflictions of the poor . . . must be redeemed" and that "we must share their lives, because it is only by becoming one with them that we can save them, that is bring God to them and bring them to God."[31]

Suffering Is Not a Value in Itself

Although Christ alone is the savior, believers through their faith become sharers in Christ's sufferings and instruments of his saving work. Paul does not hesitate to say that he has "become all things" to all "that I might by all means save some" (1 Cor 9:22). The believer is consoled in his or her sufferings by the thought that any suffering can be joined to the sufferings of Jesus and become a way of bringing salvation to others. Suffering in itself, as Mother Teresa observes, is of no value, but when it is united to the suffering of Jesus it becomes salvific. It is true that when Paul spoke of completing through his sufferings what was lacking in the passion of Christ, he was thinking of the persecutions that resulted from his preaching. But the saints in their wisdom have come to understand that any suffering borne in union with Christ's suffering is transformed into a means of bringing salvation to others. It is, of course, a complete deformation of this "saintly wisdom" to use it as an excuse for not seeking to alleviate suffering wherever it is to be found. On the contrary, the follower of Jesus, like Jesus himself, always seeks to bring healing and freedom from suffering whenever possible. But when unavoidable suffering comes, the Christian is not like those who have no hope. Rather, the disciple of Jesus the savior can rejoice, even in the midst of suffering, because he or she understands that through the "divine foolishness" of the cross suffering itself can be transformed into a source of life for oneself and others.

If it is true that Jesus can help us to bring good out of any suffering, no matter how meaningless it may appear, it is equally true that both in his earthly ministry and throughout the history of the church Jesus has offered gifts of healing from physical and psychological diseases to countless individuals. Perhaps the most frequent way believers come to a deep, heart-felt appreciation of Jesus as healer is by experiencing his healing power at work in themselves or directly witnessing its transformative effects in others. My own discovery of Jesus as healer came in personal struggles with addiction and psychological woundedness. My encounter with Jesus as healer is an ongoing affair of heart, mind, spirit. I have given an account of this journey elsewhere and I will not repeat its twists and turns here.[32] I will only refer to personal experiences in those instances where I think doing so may help illuminate some special aspect of Jesus' reality as healer of the wounded psyche.

Jesus, then, not only offered the gift of forgiveness of sins to those he encountered in his ministry. He also frequently cured individuals of physical and what we now speak of as emotional illnesses. Of course, for Jesus himself everything he did was related to his basic announcement of the good news of the reality of the kingdom. He "regarded his cures of the sick as a sign of the arrival and the beginning of the visible dawning of God's reign."[33]

There is no evidence that Jesus made physical and psychological healings the chief focus of his ministry. But when John the Baptist sent his disciples to Jesus to ask if he was the expected one, Jesus replied: "Go and tell John what you hear and see: the blind receive their sight and the lame walk, lepers are cleansed and the deaf hear . . ." (Mt 11:4–5). Clearly, Jesus, as portrayed in the gospels, saw his healings as one basic sign that with his ministry the reign of God was at hand.

The Kingdom: A Present and Future Reality

When we look at Jesus' healing ministry in the light of his death and resurrection we see that all of Jesus' physical healings were transient. As far as we know everyone Jesus healed of a physical illness eventually died. We need to view the physical healings Jesus effected as signs of the *beginning*, but not of the *consummation* of the reign of God among us. As Karl Rahner observes: "God's grace promises its power to the whole [person], in his [or her] body and soul, and if it here and now heals in passing, it is essentially intended to make it credible for [human beings] that it will heal and transfigure [them] finally when the consummation dawns in the passing through death."[34]

Jesus in the gospels tells his disciples to go forth and teach all nations (Mt 28:19) and that "they will lay their hands on the sick, and they will recover" (Mk 16:18). Jesus also tells all Christians to visit the sick (cf. Mt 25:36). There is room in the Christian church for a variety of healing charisms. There are, for example, those who are given particular gifts for healing those physically or psychologically ill. There are likewise those who are given special vocations to care for the sick, the handicapped, the dying. We see, for example, Christians like Matthew and Dennis Linn, who have special charisms for healing those physically and psychologically ill. We also see persons like Jean Vanier and his followers who have a particular vocation to work with the mentally handicapped. Again, we see Mother Teresa and her companions who are called in a special way to assist and comfort the abandoned dying and other particularly needy individuals.

The Final Suffering: Death

Those who in the name of Jesus the healer effect physical and psychological cures in an extraordinary way give powerful witness to the dynamic presence of the kingdom of God among us here and now. Those who care for the dying remind Christians, among other things, that it is only through dying that human beings enter into the fullness of the kingdom of God. Clearly, both those charisms which are given for the restoration of health in persons sick in body or mind and those which are bestowed for the comforting of the sick, who remain unhealed, and the dying are needed in the church. They each reveal a different dimension of Jesus the healer.

Jesus in his lifetime through his gift of divine forgiveness and his healings of the sick in body and mind gave witness to the presence of the loving kindness and the reign of God among us. But Jesus through his suffering and death gifted us with a healing example of how to face our own unavoidable sufferings and how to die, inwardly strengthened by the Spirit, in a godly and victorious way. Finally, Jesus revealed through his death and resurrection that "here we have no lasting city" (Heb 13:14), but that the fullness of the reign of God is present only in the resurrection from the dead when "creation itself will be set free from its bondage to decay and obtain the glorious liberty of the children of God" (Rom 8:21).

Although the unavoidable fact of death creates a discontinuity, a break between the present and final stages of the kingdom, the greater reality of love establishes an even deeper unity or bond between the two phases of the kingdom. Unfortunately, some Christians have at times so fixed their gaze on the heaven that is to come that they have reduced the present life to a pain-filled journey simply to be endured, instead of viewing it as a time to bring Jesus' healing and liberating touch to as many suffering people as possible. This false attitude led Marxists to view religion as an opiate, as a promise of future bliss that dulls people's awareness of their present misery and pain, but does nothing to improve their earthly lot. The irony in all this is that Jesus in the gospels makes entry into the fullness of the kingdom, prepared before the foundation of the world, dependent on how we dealt with the hungry, the thirsty, the sick, the naked, the imprisoned (Mt 25:31–46). What is so authentically Christian about such healers as Jean Vanier and Mother Teresa is that their deep faith in the final resurrection of all does not diminish but, in fact, deepens their desire to bring the healing touch of Jesus to all who suffer in the present.

Misuse of the Consolations of Religion

The fact that some misuse the consolations of religion as a form of escapism should not deter individuals from prayerfully seeking healing and comforting from Jesus Christ. Dorothy Day, for example, at the beginnings of her conversion to Catholicism, was so steeped in the Marxist's critique of religion as an opiate, that when she found herself praying she had to tell herself: "I am praying because I am happy, not because I am unhappy. I did not turn to God in unhappiness, in grief, in despair—to get consolation, to get something from Him."[35] Yet Jesus, in the gospel of Matthew, extends the healing invitation: "Come to me, all who labor and are heavy laden, and I will give you rest" (11:28). And Paul in 2 Corinthians refers to the Father of Jesus as the "God of all comfort, who comforts us in all our affliction, so that we may be able to comfort those who are in any affliction, with the comfort with which we ourselves are comforted by God" (2 Cor 1:4).

Many holy persons, who are outstanding in their devotion to the healing of others, first needed to experience the healing touch of Jesus in their own lives before they were able effectively to bring Jesus' gifts of healing to others. Jean Vanier forthrightly acknowledges: "I must admit that it was only when I had touched my own misery and the hatred within me that I was able to be touched by the mercy of God and discover the mystery of Jesus, gentle healer of hearts."[36] And he adds significantly: "It was only then that I was able myself to touch with a compassionate heart, the misery of others without crushing them."[37]

Jean Vanier and the Healing Christ

As I have read the books of Jean Vanier and learned from others of his awesome dedication to the mentally handicapped, I have come to appreciate deeply his role in the world as a Christ-healer. I have not come across anyone who expresses a basic "theology of Christian healing" with greater simplicity and depth of insight. Vanier has a doctorate in philosophy, but his encounters with God's little ones have led him to see the dangers in intellectual pursuits. They can be helpful, but all too often "the acquisitions of university degrees can be flight from people—a desire to become conscious of our own power and knowledge."[38] As a person with academic degrees I know only too well how accurate Vanier is in his warnings about the dangers of intellectualism. Vanier again and again stresses the need for humility, the need to be open to the experience of Jesus' healing touch in one's own life: "Jesus the Healer comes when we are conscious that we need a healer."[39]

Vanier echoes Jesus and Paul when he says that it is not to the wise and self-sufficient of this world but to little ones that he reveals himself: "When we become conscious of our own poverty, our lack of fidelity, our fears . . . then Jesus will reveal Himself as the quiet and gentle Healer."[40] I would like to reflect on some aspects of Vanier's life and writings which I think beautifully exemplify what being healed and healing in Jesus' name are all about.

Vanier and Dorothy Day

Holy people are attracted to holy people and draw inspiration from one another. Saints beget saints in Christ. Vanier recounts a visit he had with Dorothy Day. "She lives in an area where there have been several murders recently," yet "her house is always open to the out-of-work, to beggars, to poor of all kinds."[41] She is "dressed very poorly, and her face is lined with years of struggle. But her eyes are illuminated by the living love which dwells in her."[42] Holy people, of course, do not see themselves as holy, but as constantly in need of deeper spiritual growth. Dorothy Day not too long before she died wrote somewhat humorously of a visit she had made to the Rochester House of Hospitality, which reminded her of her own need for fuller spiritual freedom: "I must cultivate holy indifference. I should rejoice that I am 'just an old woman,' as the little boy said at the Rochester House of Hospitality long ago. He said, 'all day long they said, "Dorothy Day is coming," and now she's here and she's just an old woman!' "[43]

Vanier and Mother Teresa

The spiritual qualities of a "living love" and deep humility also radiate from Mother Teresa, whom Jean Vanier met in Bombay. Vanier recounts that he found his meeting with Mother Teresa a kind of "miracle."[44] Mother Teresa, a very practical lover of human beings, just as Vanier also is, remarked to him that "when you are faced with countless lepers and poor people dying by the dozen . . . there are no problems to *discuss* because there just isn't time for that."[45] Vanier in reflecting afterward on his visit to India said: "Many beautiful and wounded faces are engraved on my heart—the face of the man lying on the street . . . the sick woman begging—her child also sick, in her arms . . . the eyes and the spirit of Mother Teresa, and the simple beauty of the novices of her Order, the Missionaries of Charity, with whom I spoke of Jesus."[46] It is the radiant eyes of Dorothy Day and Mother Teresa that Vanier recalls in reflecting on his encounters with these two saints of our time. In the great spiritual traditions radiant eyes are a symbol of deep spiritual vision.

What stands out most strikingly in both Jean Vanier and Mother Teresa is that they are equally energized from the very core of their being by an intimate love of Jesus that overflows into an exquisitely warm, healing embrace of the most ignored, rejected members of humanity. Mother Teresa tells the sisters of the group she founded: "Seek Him. . . . Love Him trustfully. . . . Believe that Jesus and Jesus alone is life."[47] But Mother Teresa sees the intimate love of Jesus as a generative love. She cites Thérèse of Lisieux who said: "When I act and think charitably, I feel it is Jesus working in me; the deeper my union with Him, the stronger my love for the residents of Carmel."[48] For Thérèse of Lisieux her daily contact with others was generally limited to the sisters with whom she lived in Carmel. But the sisters of Mother Teresa's society are called to the apostolic service of loving and healing the poorest of the poor. Mother Teresa exhorts her sisters to be "true co-workers of Christ"; to "radiate and live His life"; to be "angel[s] of comfort to the sick"[49] and with the eyes of faith to behold Jesus, "the most beautiful One in those broken with pain and suffering."[50]

A Tender, Generative Love

In close spiritual kinship with Mother Teresa, Jean Vanier in his writings constantly reveals a deep, tender love of Jesus that overflows into a healing love of the most needy of God's children. Vanier, for example, in talks he gave to leaders of religious orders asked them: "Is it true that you believe Jesus loves you? Is it true that you have a personal relationship with Him?"[51] Vanier then told the superiors, in the simple, poetic language so characteristic of him:

So it all begins from this
  When I discover
    how much He loves
      me

  and that He calls me,
    tenderly,
      by name

then

I will be able to love
  you, my brother
  you, my sister

as He loves you;
tenderly,
    calling forth Jesus in you.[52]

Some might object that the warm, tender love of Jesus, which
characterizes the spirituality of Mother Teresa and Jean Vanier, is
not appropriate for the new generation of Christian believers. But
if this is the case, it is difficult to explain the large numbers of
young followers these two holy people continuously attract to
their apostolates. Also, if it is true that we know the tree from its
fruits, then we must acknowledge the excellence and spiritual
fertility of a deep, intimate love of Jesus, since this very love is the
interior dynamo that has provided the world with two of the most
outstanding servants of wounded humanity in our time.

Jean Vanier through his experiences in his l'Arche communities
of the mentally handicapped has also come to a profound understanding of the healing value of communities gathered in the name
of Jesus. Jesus said that "where two or three are gathered in my
name, there am I in the midst of them" (Mt 18:20). Vanier acknowledges that "the revelation of the love of God almost always
comes through a relationship with someone, and in the heart of a
community."[53] But he also stresses that mentally handicapped individuals have a very special need to experience the personal love
of Jesus. There is no guarantee that any one specific person will
always be physically available to another. And the community, *as
community*, cannot satisfy the radical human need for lasting one-
to-one personal encounters. "Someone having a mental handicap,
who is sometimes so limited and whose heart is so full of suffering,
has a greater need than anyone else to encounter Jesus."[54]

The Experience of a Burning Heart

Vanier attests to a unique experience of God, the "experience of
a burning heart," which is given to many children and handicapped individuals. This "experience of a burning heart" is the
experience of the absolute, unconditioned love of God. "In that
love which burns, illuminates and enlivens the heart, one discovers that one is precious to God just as one is, in one's very
being"; all of us, but especially the children and mentally handicapped, "need to have confidence in the absolute of a relationship
with Jesus."[55] Vanier says that although many "adults" do not
believe in such experiences, they are a fact. He emphasizes that

even healthy married couples need the experience of the absolute love of Jesus because all human beings are limited and cannot be "God for one another."[56] When either the mentally handicapped or the so-called "average person" experiences the absolute, unconditioned love of God, of Jesus, then he or she is able to live with the uncertainties, flaws, sinfulness and limitations that characterize all finite, interpersonal relationships. "When we discover that we are loved with an eternal love, with a love beyond all time and space, which goes even beyond death, then everything begins to change, all becomes possible, all can be accepted and loved."[57]

The Illusion of Perfect Healing

Vanier also warns against an idealism, rampant today, which operates out of the dangerous illusion that "everyone may become perfectly healed and find perfect unity"; he says that ever "new therapies engender more and better illusions," but that he grows more and more convinced "that there is not perfect healing," that "each human being carries his own wounds, his own difficulties of relationship and his own anguishes," and that, finally, it is a matter of learning "to accept who we are" and of living "with what we have, focusing our strength on those others who are in greater need and sometimes in deep distress."[58] My own experiences of the last few years tend to validate for me Vanier's claim that "there is not perfect healing" this side of the resurrection from the dead. In reflecting on my own earliest writings on Jesus as healer, especially as healer of the wounded psyche, I see that at times I was overly optimistic about the completeness of such healings.

We move falteringly in this life toward the ideal of perfect integration in Christ. We are best off, as Karl Rahner observes, when we let go of ourselves and entrust ourselves, together with our "fears and cares and . . . illness," to God; then, our "illness, even when it remains, loses its senselessness."[59] And, paradoxically, our letting go of our fear of not being healed puts us in the best state of mind and heart for a healing of some kind to occur. Also, when we do seek the comforting and healing of Jesus we do so more and more out of a desire to be of help to others in even greater distress, "so that we may be able to comfort those who are in any affliction, with the comfort with which we ourselves are comforted by God" (2 Cor 1:4). In this way our deep, personal love of Jesus the healer becomes a generative love, which seeks to make the healing touch of Jesus, the healer, present to others.

Notes

1. Karl Rahner, *The Love of Jesus and the Love of Neighbor* (New York: Crossroad, 1983), p. 23.

2. Cf. Bernard Tyrrell, *Christotherapy* (New York: Paulist Press, 1986), esp. pp. 164–181 and *Christotherapy II* (New York: Paulist Press, 1982), esp. pp. 145–233.

3. Karl Rahner, "Christmas, the Festival of Eternal Youth," *Theological Investigations, Vol. VII,* translated by David Bourke (New York: Herder and Herder, 1971), p. 121.

4. Catherine de Hueck Dougherty, *Molchanie: The Silence of God* (New York: Crossroad, 1982), p. 89.

5. Walter Kasper, *Jesus the Christ* (New York: Paulist Press, 1976).

6. Jean Vanier, *Man and Woman He Made Them* (New York: Paulist Press, 1985), p. 18.

7. Ibid.

8. Ibid.

9. Ibid., p. 23.

10. Ibid., p. 34.

11. C. G. Jung, *Memories, Dreams, Reflections,* edited by Aniela Jaffe and translated by Richard and Clara Winston (New York: Vintage Books, 1965), p. 9.

12. Ibid., pp. 11–15.

13. Ibid., pp. 13–14.

14. Vital Jourdain, *The Heart of Father Damien,* translated from the French by Francis Larkin and Charles Davenport (Milwaukee: Bruce Publishing Company, 1955), p. 238.

15. Ibid., p. 30.

16. Ibid., p. 243.

17. Ibid., pp. 344–345.

18. John Donne, *The Complete Poetry and Selected Prose of John Donne,* with an introduction by Robert Silliman Hillyer (New York: Modern Library of Random House, 1941), p. 272.

19. Karl Rahner, "Faith as Courage," *Theological Investigations, Vol. XVIII,* translated by Edward Quinn (New York: Crossroad, 1983), p. 218.

20. Catherine de Hueck Doherty, *The Gospel Without Compromise* (Notre Dame, Indiana: Ave Maria Press, 1976), p. 137.

21. Julian of Norwich, *Julian of Norwich—Showings,* translated and introduced by Edmund Colledge, O.S.A. and James Walsh, S.J. (New York: Paulist Press, 1978), p. 279.

22. Ibid., p. 221.

23. Karl Rahner, "Unity—Love—Mystery," *Theological Investigations, Vol. VIII,* translated by David Bourke (New York: Herder and Herder, 1971), p. 240.

24. Ibid., p. 241.

25. Dorothy Day, *Therese* (Notre Dame, Indiana: Fides Publishers, 1960), p. 175.

26. Ibid., pp. 175–176.

27. Oscar Romero, *Voice of the Voiceless* (Maryknoll, New York: Orbis Books, 1985), p. 70.

28. Ibid.

29. Mother Teresa, *The Love of Christ,* edited by George Gorree and Jean Barbier (San Francisco: Harper and Row, 1982), p. 58.

30. Ibid.

31. Ibid., pp. 58–59.

32. Cf. Bernard Tyrrell, *Christotherapy,* esp. ix–xviii and *Christotherapy II,* esp. pp. 1–9.

33. Karl Rahner, "The Saving Force and Healing Power of Faith," *Theological Investigations, Vol. V.,* translated by Karl-H. Krugwe (Baltimore: Helicon Press, 1966), p. 463.

34. Ibid., p. 467.

35. Dorothy Day, *The Long Loneliness* (New York: Harper and Brothers, 1952), pp. 132–133.

36. Jean Vanier, *Man and Woman He Made Them* (New York: Paulist Press, 1985), p. 173.

37. Ibid.

38. Jean Vanier, *Be Not Afraid* (New York: Paulist Press, 1975), p. 39.

39. Ibid.

40. Ibid., p. 47.

41. Ibid., p. 5.

42. Ibid.

43. Dorothy Day, *By Little and By Little* (New York: Alfred Knopf, 1983), p. 360.

44. Jean Vanier, *Followers of Jesus* (New York: Paulist Press, 1976), p. 6.

45. Ibid.

46. Ibid., ix.

47. Mother Teresa, *The Love of Christ,* p. 75.

48. Ibid., p. 44.

49. Ibid., p. 67.

50. Ibid., p. 109.

51. Jean Vanier, *Followers of Jesus,* p. 46.

52. Ibid., p. 76.

53. Jean Vanier, *Man and Woman He Made Them,* p. 114.

54. Ibid.

55. Ibid., pp. 24–25.

56. Ibid., p. 24.

57. Ibid., p. 114.

58. Ibid., p. 61.

59. Karl Rahner, "The Saving Force and Healing Power of Faith," *Theological Investigations, Vol. V,* pp. 464–465.

Liberator of Captives, the Poor, the Oppressed

If Jesus sought to console and heal the sick in body and mind, he also, like Amos and other Hebrew prophets before him, showed a special concern for the poor and the social outcasts of his world. In Luke Jesus inaugurates his public ministry by applying to himself the words of the prophet Isaiah:

The Spirit of the Lord is upon me,
because he has anointed me to preach good news to the poor.
He has sent me to proclaim release to the captives
and recovering of sight to the blind,
to set at liberty those who are oppressed . . . (Lk 4:18).

Jesus was open to everyone in his ministry, but he fulfilled the words of Isaiah by daily showing a particular care for the destitute, the despised, the abused, the exploited, the most helpless members of his society.

Our focus on the image of Jesus as liberator gives rise to a number of key questions which can serve as guideposts in reflecting on Jesus the liberator. When did the image of Jesus as liberator become a central image for a large number of Christians? Do believers attracted by the vision of Jesus as liberator find in him basically a model for the liberation of whole peoples or rather of small groups and particular individuals suffering from various forms of oppression? Does the love of Jesus as liberator lead Christians to strive to free others, as Jesus did, or does an encounter with the oppressed and outcasts impel believers to turn to Jesus as liberator and to seek from him inspiration and strength in their quest to liberate others? What are the catalysts that awaken in Christians a vital interest in issues of liberation, an ever deepening love of Jesus as liberator and a desire to liberate as Jesus liberates? What are the feelings that burn in the heart of Jesus the liberator and animate his followers in their quest for the total liberation of humankind from every form of oppression, discrimination, enslavement?

Emergence of "Jesus the Liberator" as a Key Image

When, then, did the image of Jesus as liberator become a central image for a large number of Christians? Clearly, each age has its own particular sufferings as well as achievements, and Christian believers inevitably look on Jesus, as he reveals himself in scripture, through the prism of the agonies and ecstasies of the period in which they live. Jaroslav Pelikan observes that, although in Jesus' own time and ever since there has existed a tradition of describing him as liberator, it is above all in the nineteenth and twentieth centuries that "the first century Prophet who had preached the justice of God as it was directed against all the oppressors of humanity" has become "Jesus the Liberator."[1] Mohandas Gandhi was profoundly influenced by Jesus' teachings on love in his quest for the liberation of his people from colonial oppression through the use of non-violent resistance. More recently, Martin Luther King found in Jesus' sermon on the mount and his teachings on love a major source of inspiration in his nonviolent struggle for the liberation of American blacks. Pelikan recounts that when a renowned scholar of black literature in America was queried as to why Martin Luther King did not become a Marxist he replied: "Because of the overpowering force of the figure of Jesus."[2]

Jesus: Liberator of Individuals or Groups?

Next, the question arises: Do believers attracted by the vision of Jesus as liberator find in him basically a model for the liberation of whole peoples or rather of small groups and particular individuals suffering from various forms of oppression? There is, in fact, no "either/or" answer to this question. Jesus himself is portrayed in the New Testament as feeling compassion for the multitudes (Mk 6:34) *and* for particular individuals (Mk 1:41). Jesus is also described as weeping for his people, for Jerusalem (Lk 19:41) *and* for an individual, his friend Lazarus (Jn 11:35).

Today we find followers of Jesus who have compassion for economically and politically oppressed groups and who speak out in the name of Jesus the liberator against the injustices perpetrated by the powerful against the poor. The slain Archbishop Oscar Romero of El Salvador is a striking example of a Christian believer who, like Jesus, had compassion on the multitudes and sought justice for the poor, even at the risk of his life. In similar fashion, Bishop Pedro Casaldaliga of Brazil, a friend of Oscar Romero, continues to this day to imitate the martyred bishop in speaking out, even in the face of death threats, against economic and political injustice.

But God has also raised up those followers of Jesus who have felt compassion for specific individuals suffering from poverty, discrimination and abuse and who have sought on a local and even one-to-one level to liberate these persons from their sufferings or at least to alleviate their pain. Damien of Molokai is a good example of a holy person who in his work for the lepers on Molokai sought to free them from the discrimination practiced against them, to provide adequate shelter, clothing, food for them and a sense of dignity. Dorothy Day and her mentor and friend, Peter Maurin, also strove through the establishment of their Hospitality Houses to provide immediate assistance on the local level for hungry and needy individuals. They also attempted through their publication, *The Catholic Worker*, to secure on a more long-range basis a just wage and dignity for working persons. Mother Teresa likewise seeks to aid poor individuals directly through the works of her Missionary Sisters and Brothers of Charity. The latter take a special vow of free, wholehearted service to the poor. What we see is that there are many ways and many diverse social levels at which disciples of Jesus the liberator can and do imitate him in his quest to aid the poor and to set at liberty those who are oppressed.

A further question presents itself: Which comes first? Does the love of Jesus as liberator lead Christians to strive to free others, as Jesus did, or does an encounter with the oppressed and outcasts impel believers to look to Jesus as liberator and to seek from him inspiration and strength in the quest to free others from bondage?

Love of the Liberating Jesus
and the Longing To Liberate

In the case of Damien of Molokai we have an example of an individual who undertook his mission to the outcasts out of love for Christ and with the desire to imitate his Lord in his desire to preach the good news and to help those who suffer. Damien wrote: "We should give ourselves to all, without exception, without reserve. The measure of our zeal should be that of Jesus Christ."[3] But Damien was also moved with deep compassion for his lepers. He wrote to his religious superior: "I am in the midst of moral and physical miseries that break my heart. However, I always try to appear happy in order to keep up my poor lepers' courage."[4] Damien did not explicitly look upon himself as a follower of Jesus *as liberator,* but, in fact, he did fight for the rights and dignity of his lepers and to free them from the degrading poverty and misery they daily experienced.

Damien was most certainly drawn to serve the poor out of love for Jesus. But in his work for the liberation of his lepers from their awful suffering he felt the need to have recourse to Jesus for inspiration and strength. He wrote at a time of great internal suffering: "Without the constant presence of our Divine Master in my poor chapel, I could not go on living my life here with the lepers of Molokai." Yet, "having Our Lord near me, I am always happy and have the drive to work for the good of my dear lepers."[5] Damien sought to liberate his lepers out of love for Christ, but he was also moved to aid his lepers out of profound love and compassion for them.

Dorothy Day's Secular and Christian Liberating Loves

In striking contrast to Fr. Damien, Dorothy Day was dedicated to the service of the poor long before she embraced the cause and person of Jesus. But, once converted, she wrote that she and her companions on the staff of the *Catholic Worker* "felt a respect for the poor and destitute as those nearest to God, as those chosen by Christ for His compassion."[6] Dorothy Day came to discover in Jesus *the* liberator of the poor and oppressed. She wrote of Jesus that "He directed His sublime words to the poorest of the poor, to the people . . . who hung around, sick and poverty-stricken at the doors of rich men."[7] She stated bluntly that Jesus "had set us an example and the poor and destitute were the ones we wished to reach."[8] And, like Damien, Dorothy Day too found strength and support in Jesus Christ. She wrote of the "lively realization that there is such a thing as the love of Christ for us"[9] and that "we can turn to our Lord Jesus Christ . . . and trust that He will make up for our falls, for our neglects, our failures in love."[10]

Most certainly, the Holy Spirit guided Dorothy Day and Damien of Molokai along very different spiritual paths, but in the end they both loved the poor, loved Jesus in the poor and the poor because of Jesus. Damien of Molokai was led through his love of Jesus to serve his poor lepers, especially the children, to the point of becoming a leper himself. He wrote: "My greatest happiness is to serve the Lord in these poor sick children."[11] Dorothy Day found her "secular" love of the poor transformed and enriched through her conversion to the love of Jesus, who identified himself with the poorest of the poor. For Damien and for Day the love of Jesus and of the neighbor were one. Day wrote: "We cannot love God unless we love each other, and to love we must know each other." She added: "We know Him in the breaking of the bread, and we know each other in the breaking of the bread, and we are not alone any more."[12]

Next, we ask: What are some of the catalysts that can awaken in us an awareness and love of Jesus as liberator and a desire to bring freedom to outcasts, to the poor and oppressed, as Jesus did?

Jesus' Unconditioned Love of the Wretched

In my case, I first began to understand with my heart something of the reality of Jesus as liberator of impoverished and socially ostracized persons in my pilgrim journey toward sobriety with other alcoholic brothers and sisters. I met people who were poor in every sense of the word. I came to realize that their economic and other forms of poverty were not necessarily the result of willful, clear-eyed decisions and that, in any case, this was not the decisive issue. God loves the impoverished, not because they are good or deserving, but precisely because they are poor, because they are needy, because they are wretched.[13] What stands out for me most strikingly about the way Jesus dealt with the socially ostracized of his society—the man born blind, lepers, and others—is that, despite their wretched condition, he treated them with respect. He was at ease in their presence and spontaneously conferred on them a sense of self-worth and dignity as children of his beloved abba.

A Preferential Love of Outcasts

As I walk along the streets in typical American cities and am approached by derelicts, by beggars, by alcoholics, I have to remind myself that these are the very type of people toward whom Jesus showed a most special love and concern. He did not shy away from them. He was not condescending in his approach to them. Rather, he proclaimed them blessed and welcomed them into the kingdom of the abba. In fact, he told certain chief priests and elders of the people: "Truly, I say to you, the tax collectors and the harlots go into the kingdom of God before you" (Mt 21:31).

One "happy" result of my struggle with alcoholism is that I have come to the deep realization that I am no better than the derelict I meet by chance on the street. I thus find that a good barometer of how much I have truly made my own the mind and heart of Jesus the liberator is the way I respond now to the down and out whom I encounter. Do I treat them with respect or in a patronizing manner? Do I immediately tend to judge and blame them in my mind for the wretched condition they are in or am I inclined rather to give them the benefit of the doubt and to extend a helping hand? Clearly, there are times when we need to show a "tough" kind of love toward the addict, the derelict, the prostitute. But a "tough" love is still a love that acknowledges the dignity of the person and that does all it can to seek the liberation of the wretched one from his or her particular misery and captivity.

Each of us, of course, is awakened to the reality and call of Jesus the liberator in the unique circumstances of his or her own particular life situation. Clearly, the "catalyst" that initially and powerfully opened my eyes to the reality of Jesus as liberator of captives was my struggle with alcoholic addiction and my ensuing encounter with so many impoverished and often despised outcasts in our contemporary society. In my misery I looked to Jesus for assistance and I gradually came to see through contemplating Jesus in holy scripture that he had a special, preferential love for outcasts of all sorts and that in him I had hope. As I slowly recovered I experienced Jesus the liberator at work in my recovery process and I came to love him as my liberator and the liberator of other addicts as well. I also experienced an inner calling to follow Jesus in his quest to liberate captives by seeking to do what I could to liberate addicts and others from whatever misery, poverty, degradation that holds them in bondage.

The key feelings that Jesus, liberator of the outcasts, the addicts, the socially ostracized, evokes in those he frees from bondage are feelings of deep love, gratitude and confidence in him. These liberated individuals likewise experience feelings of deepening

respect and esteem for themselves as beloved children of God and
an inner serenity and peace they had not previously known.

Learning from the Exploited and Oppressed

A second major catalyst in my discovery of Jesus as liberator of
the oppressed has been my encounters with women in my pastoral
activities of spiritual direction and counseling and in other ways as
well. In my ongoing dialogues with women friends, directees, relatives and students I have gradually become aware of the massive, if
at times subtle, forms of oppression of women that exist on all levels
of American society and worldwide. I realize, of course, that it is,
above all, the oppressed, who know what the pain of enslavement is
really like. Who, for example, can fully understand the pain of a
woman from a third world country who described herself as oppressed and impoverished in six ways: as a woman, as a prostitute, as
a single parent, as black, as poor, as a person from a despised
tribe?[14] I cannot begin to comprehend the agony of this woman.

Yet, second only to the personal experience of oppression is an
encounter and dialogue with oppressed individuals and groups.
And I am immensely grateful to the women whom I have encountered in spiritual guidance, in classes and elsewhere, who have
helped me understand in some small measure the pain, sharp or
numbing, that women experience in the face of manifold forms of
discrimination and exploitation. It is also from these women, above
all, that I have learned to discover Jesus as liberator of women, as
one who stood on the side of oppressed women in his day and who
is a beacon of hope for all who in our day seek the liberation of
women from all forms of discrimination.

Reading as a Catalyst of Enlightenment

Another powerful catalyst for discovering Jesus as liberator of
the oppressed—women and others—is reading. We need only
think of the tremendous impact Augustine's reading of a passage
from Paul and Ignatius of Loyola's reading of the lives of the saints
had on their lives. Today men and women are reading holy scripture to see in what ways it might shed new light on the various
struggles currently going on throughout the world for the liberation of oppressed individuals and groups.

I have found a special consolation and challenge in the written
reflections of contemporary women on the attitude of Jesus to-

ward women and his interactions with them as depicted in the gospels. Rosemary Haughton, for example, to name but one current author, outstanding in her work for the poor, offers unique insights in her written reflections on Jesus and his relationships with the women of his day.

Rosemary Haughton has worked for some years as a member of Wellspring House, a center of hospitality for the homeless and a training place for individuals who feel called to serve the poor of North America. Most of the guests at Wellspring are "women, women who have suffered abuse of every kind." These women "are not unlike the prostitutes, the adulteresses, the desperate women with sick children whom Jesus encountered and to whose need and pain he responded with openness and deep compassion."[15] Rosemary Haughton's recent writing shows "the kind of reflection in which there is an interplay between the experience of contemporary women and the experiences of the 'women with Jesus' and those in the young church."[16]

Liberation: A Passionate Commitment

Some readers of Rosemary Haughton—and other authors like her—will be put off by the passion and at times anger she reveals when she contrasts the way many Christians treat women today with the way Jesus dealt with them. Rosemary Haughton, like Dorothy Day, is a woman who can take a strong passionate approach to issues that touch her most deeply. But then Haughton and Day have both tried to follow Jesus, about whom Day wrote: "When I think of Jesus I think of someone who was *constantly* passionate. . . . His whole life was a Passion . . . [an] energy."[17]

It is possible to benefit deeply from the writings of such women as Dorothy Day and Rosemary Haughton without necessarily agreeing with them on all points. One can admire and learn much from Dorothy Day, for example, without embracing her radical pacifism, just as one can venerate Oscar Romero as a very holy man, perhaps a saint, without necessarily espousing his views on the legitimacy of using force against an unlawfully constituted government. The most important thing is that these holy people through their lives and writings prod us to reflect prayerfully on how Jesus dealt with oppressed persons and groups and to ask how we ourselves measure up, as disciples of Jesus, liberator of the poor, the marginal, the outcast.

Jesus and his Encounters with Women

It is most illuminating to ponder scriptural passages from a new perspective and with new questions. This is one way the householder can bring new things as well as old out of the treasury (Mt 13:52). I have found it extremely profitable to meditate on those biblical passages where Jesus encounters women and to ask what attitudes he reveals, what actions he takes. Rosemary Haughton and others have helped me greatly in this prayerful enterprise. Here I can only cite a few examples and urge the reader to engage in similar kinds of reflections on Jesus in his dealings with women. I should also add, as Rosemary Haughton does, that there are at times opposing interpretations of the scriptural passages dealing with Jesus in his relationship with women, as there are of other scriptural texts. So the textual interpretations I offer are tentative and subject to correction. And the final discerner in these matters is the church.

But if there is anything that stands out clearly about Jesus in his relationships with women, it is that he treated them with a respect and dignity that often stood in sharp contrast to his contemporaries in their approach to women. Thus Jesus' own closest disciples are disturbed when they find him conversing with the Samaritan woman at the well: "Just then his disciples came. They marveled that he was talking with a woman, but none said, 'What do you wish?' or 'Why are you talking with her?' " (Jn 4:27). Again, in the time of Jesus a man could easily divorce his wife, but not vice versa. But Jesus taught that a husband was required to remain faithful until death to his wife, just as she was also called to remain faithful to him (Mk 10:2–12). And, in the case of the woman caught in adultery, Jesus pointed out the hypocrisy of her male accusers by suggesting that the man among them who was without sin—perhaps sexual sin—should cast the first stone.[18] Again, a woman with a hemorrhage, who was viewed as unclean and as polluting everyone with whom she came in contact, reached out in the midst of a pressing crowd and touched Jesus. He did not complain because she touched him, but he healed her and praised her faith: "Daughter, your faith has made you well; go in peace, and be healed of your disease" (Mk 5:34).[19]

Jesus: A Man for Women

As Rosemary Haughton observes, "it must have been extremely difficult for Jesus to be male in the kind of society into which he was born."[20] Jesus refused to let social, sexual, political categories dictate the quality of his relationships with women or men. He invited everyone to share table-community with him, to enter into the kingdom, to become his disciples. The gospel of Luke describes Mary, the sister of Martha as " 'sitting at the feet' of Jesus, which was a technical phrase referring to the stance of the accredited disciple toward a Master, as Saul 'sat at the feet' of the great Rabbi Gamaliel."[21] Jesus delighted in the company and friendship of women as well as men. Jesus' presence was a kind, nurturing, deeply "incarnate" presence. He often healed through touching, and he had the highest praise for the "woman of the city" who came into a banquet Jesus was attending and, "standing behind him at his feet, weeping . . . began to wet his feet with her tears, and wiped them with the hair of her head, and kissed his feet, and anointed them with ointment" (Lk 7:38). Far from telling this unclean woman, this sinner, to desist from touching him, Jesus praised her great love and said to her: "Your faith has saved you; go in peace" (Lk 7:50).

Jesus was most certainly a liberator of women from oppression in his time, and he remains as *the* liberator par excellence of women today. He provides a model for men who seek to be freed from all forms of sexism and discriminatory practices toward women. He reveals to women that it is possible for a male to be truly not only a "man for others" but a "man for women" in total dedication to their liberation from all forms of exploitation, discrimination, oppression.

I am immensely grateful to Rosemary Haughton and other women who write with such great affection about Jesus as their champion and liberator and who reveal such a powerful love for Jesus in page after page of their writings. I find a new kind of love for Jesus arising in my own heart. I love Jesus for beginning to liberate me from my own biases and deep-set, at times scarcely conscious, oppressive attitudes and practices. I love him as a man who authentically loved women and who calls me to love with the same liberating love he possessed and now offers to me. The courage that Jesus demonstrated in confronting the prejudices and unjust practices toward women in his day inspires courage to face and overcome discriminatory, exploitative practices against women that exist today. Love, compassion, enthusiasm, courage —such is the constellation of feelings that Jesus the liberator of women evokes in the hearts of all who dare to contemplate and imitate him in his liberating attitudes and deeds.

Martyrs for Justice in the Name of Love

Perhaps the most powerful catalyst of all for awakening in a person a passionate love of Jesus as liberator of the oppressed is the example of martyrs and of individuals now alive who show a willingness to sacrifice their lives, if necessary, so that all "captives" of whatever "oppressor" "may be set free" (Lk 4:18).

Archbishop Oscar Romero is a striking example of a man who laid down his life out of love for Jesus Christ and of the poor. Bishop Pedro Cassadaliga is a living example of a man who is deeply in love with Jesus Christ and has again and again put his life on the line for the sake of the victimized poor. I focus on these two men here, not because they are bishops or because they are men, but because they embody in their lives and writings a profound commitment to Jesus the liberator and to his poor, and because of certain striking, most instructive experiences they have in common.

Oscar Romero and Rutilio Grande

Oscar Romero became archbishop of San Salvador in 1977 at a time of great unrest in his country. Shortly after he became archbishop, Fr. Rutilio Grande, S.J. and two companions, an old man and a boy, were murdered as they were on their way to celebrate mass. Fr. Grande was a close friend of Archbishop Romero. He had worked closely with the archbishop in introducing the renewal of Vatican II into the Salvadoran church. He was also outspoken in his service of the poor and oppressed. Archbishop Romero rushed to a remote place to receive the bodies of Fr. Grande and his two murdered assistants. The archbishop later often remarked that the murder of Fr. Grande was the crucial moment in his conversion to a complete dedication to the oppressed poor of his country. He began to speak out forcefully against the injustices perpetrated against the helpless by the powerful. As persecutions, tortures, murders increased, Archbishop Romero said that it was his lot "to go on claiming dead bodies," to "walk the roads gathering up dead friends, listening to widows and orphans, and trying to spread hope."[22]

In four pastoral letters to his people Romero spoke out ever more forcefully against the massive injustices, the torturing, the "disappearances," the murders of countless innocents. Romero realized that because of his strong denunciations of the rich and the powerful in the name of the poor his life was in danger. Just two weeks before his murder he said in an interview: "I have frequently been threatened with death. . . . As a pastor, I am bound by a divine command to give my life for those whom I love, and that includes all Salvadoreans, even those who are going to kill me."[23] And on March 24, 1980 the archbishop himself did become the victim of an assassin's bullet, as he was celebrating mass. Today thousands upon thousands in El Salvador venerate the slain archbishop as a saint.

Pedro Cassadaliga and Identification with the Poor

Fr. Pedro Cassadaliga was consecrated bishop of Sao Felix in the Matto Grosso in Brazil on October 23, 1971. He chose, instead of a bishop's ring and crosier, a straw hat and Indian walking stick as his episcopal emblems, to show his solidarity with the poor. He was a friend and supporter of Archbishop Romero. Bishop Cassadaliga has for many years been an ardent defender of the rights of the poor to land and a decent standard of living. His life-style is one of great poverty and simplicity. He, like Archbishop Romero, has received countless death threats, but he still lives to speak out in the name of the oppressed. Cassadaliga has, however, stared death in the face and personally witnessed the murder of an innocent. On the evening of October 11, 1976, Bishop Cassadaliga and Fr. John Burnier, S.J. went to a police station to try to stop the torture of two innocent women. A gun went off and Fr. Burnier fell, mortally wounded, at the bishop's side. This experience did not weaken Cassadaliga's commitment to the poor, but it has only deepened it. Like one of his favorite saints, Ignatius of Antioch, Bishop Cassadaliga prays that he might, if possible, receive the gift of dying for the poor. Here too he resembles Archbishop Romero who said: "Martyrdom is a grace from God that I do not believe I have earned. But if God accepts the sacrifice of my life, then may my blood be the seed of liberty."[24]

Both bishops have manifested in their lives and writings an intimate love for Jesus Christ and a desire to bring good news to the poor and to set captives free, as Jesus the liberator did. Archbishop Romero wrote that Jesus is himself "the gospel of God"[25] and that "the study and contemplation of Christ . . . should constitute the chief preoccupation of those of us who make up his church."[26] But Romero saw clearly that "one must not love oneself so much as to avoid getting involved in the risks of life that history demands of us" and that "those who out of love for Christ give themselves to the service of others will live."[27] In similar fashion, Cassadaliga writes: "I believe in [Jesus Christ] and I adore him! I love him. I live by him and for him. I would like to give my life for him. I hope, at any rate, to die in him, in order to live with him eternally."[28] And, like Damien of Molokai, Cassadaliga writes of the importance of prayer in his life and that he has not "been able to get along without visits to the Blessed Sacrament because I believe in the real sacramental presence."[29] At the same time, like Romero, Cassadaliga beholds in Jesus the liberator of the oppressed, and he stresses the need "out of love for him, for the sake of the gospel, progressively to bring about—in this first, earthly and conflict-ridden phase of his reign—the new life of the children of God, who are all equal and free, with that liberty wherein Christ liberated us" (Gal 5:1).[30]

Feelings Evoked by the Image of Jesus the Liberator

What are the feelings that the image of Jesus, the liberator, evoke in Bishops Romero and Cassadaliga? Clearly, the dominant feeling that fills the hearts of these two men is love: love of Jesus, love of the oppressed, love of the oppressors.

But love of the oppressor does not exclude the feeling of prophetic anger. Jesus, for example, expressed deep anger toward certain scribes and Pharisees when he said: "They bind heavy burdens, hard to bear, and lay them on men's shoulders; but they themselves will not move them with their finger" (Mt 23:4). Again, in the "woes" Jesus pronounced he said: "But woe to you that are rich, for you have received your consolation" (Lk 6:24).

Love and Prophetic Anger

Archbishop Romero and Bishop Pedro Cassadaliga are contemporary prophetic voices who cry out against the practices of powerful individuals and groups who have condoned or actively engaged in the systematic oppression and exploitation of the poor. Both bishops echo in their denuntiations of injustice, perpetrated at the highest levels of authority, the prophetic anger of Jesus as he spoke out against leaders in his day who abused the poor. Thus, Archbishop Romero, wrote:

> The terrible words spoken by the prophets of Israel continue to be verified among us. Among us there are those who sell others for money, who sell a poor person for a pair of sandals;

those who, in their mansions, pile up violence and plunder; those who crush the poor; those who make the kingdom of violence come closer as they lie upon their beds of ivory.[31]

And Bishop Cassadaliga writes: "Among my other passions, I have this passion of anger, I think it might be a sort of exasperated 'sacrament' of my love for my neighbor." He continues: "Setting aside my own modest anger, the anger of the prophets and the anger of Jesus were, in their own day and way, a sacrament of the inward fire and zeal for the glory of God and the dignity of man."[32] But, like Jesus, Romero and Cassadaliga both strongly reject hatred of the enemy and stress instead love and forgiveness. Romero had forgiven his murderers, even before he was struck down. And Cassadaliga writes: "Clearly, I would not even like to see a flower petal 'violated.' I am allergic to violence both by temperament and by faith." He adds: "I believe in forgiving one's enemies." "I don't think I've ever 'hated' anyone. I have never rejoiced in the death of anyone or wished anyone 'ill'."[33]

"The Strange Peace of God"

Peace is a most precious spiritual feeling of the heart, and the prayer for peace on earth among all peoples is constantly lifted up to God by persons of good will. But Jesus' words about peace and Romero's and Cassadaliga's reflections on peace reveal a profoundly paradoxical reality. In the gospel of John Jesus says: "Peace I leave with you; my peace I give to you" (Jn 14:27). In Matthew Jesus warns: "Do not think that I have come to bring peace on earth; I have not come to bring peace, but a sword" (Mt 10:34).

About peace, Romero writes: "The world of the poor teaches us what the nature of Christian love is, a love that certainly seeks peace but also unmasks false pacifism—the pacifism of resignation and inactivity."[34] Cassadaliga, a bishop who is also a poet, in one poem says to Jesus, "You are . . . My war and my peace."[35] Elsewhere, he writes: "God knows how much I have prayed and sought for *peace*," namely, "the peace I always seek; the peace I never find. The strange peace of God that bears me like some creaking, joyful boat."[36] And, like Romero, Cassadaliga warns of the dangers of an inauthentic peace: "During these days of conflict . . . the very word 'peace' smacks to me of inertia, interested complicity, and angelism."[37] Indeed, he asks: "Can anyone be

blessed for seeking peace if, at the same time, he does not seek
justice with a burning thirst?''[38]

There are, then, authentic and inauthentic forms of interior
peace and of the "peace" that can exist within nations and between peoples. For a peace to be true peace it needs to be a peace
that is active, a peace that works for ever deeper harmony within
the heart and among individuals and peoples. The poet Hopkins
expressed the paradoxical nature of peace most exquisitely in his
poem *Peace:* "And when Peace here does house He comes with
work to do, he does not come to coo, He comes to brood and sit."[39]
True peace is essentially a generative peace, a peace that like a
mother bird broods over her eggs until they are hatched and the
fledglings sent forth.

Hope and Courage

Besides the deep feelings of love, righteous anger, forgiveness,
peace, the image of Jesus the liberator also evokes in the hearts of
Romero and Cassadaliga strong feelings of hope and courage. Romero often spoke of hope.

> The real world of the poor also teaches us about Christian
> hope. The church preaches a new heaven and a new earth. It
> knows, moreover, that no socio-political system can be ex-
> changed for the final fullness that is given by God. But it has
> also learned that transcendent hope must be preserved by
> signs of hope in history, no matter how simple they may ap-
> parently be—such as those proclaimed by the Trito-Isaiah
> when he says 'they will build houses and inhabit them, plant
> vineyards and eat their fruit' (Isa. 65:21).[40]

Romero, who was renowned in his life for his courage, linked
hope and courage together. For where a person really has hope, a
hope poured into his or her heart by the Holy Spirit, that Spirit
also bestows the gift of courage to seek to bring about the object of
one's hope. "The Spirit God has given us is no cowardly spirit,
but rather one that makes us strong, loving and wise" (2 Tim
1:7 NAB).

Cassadaliga too links hope and courage. He writes that "hope
has been my credo throughout the most conscious part of my
life"[41] and that "my hope has a first and last name: JESUS-CHRIST
RISEN."[42] But he confesses that because of his psychological

makeup and the contingencies of his life "anxiety has followed me, like a shadow . . . and, many times, fear."[43] At the same time, he writes in his diary that "prayer is hope's breathing"[44] and that "the valiant are the ones who can overcome the much or little fear they have," that "the believers are those who overcome, in hope, all the doubts, the terrors and the bitternesses that necessarily invade us here, in this pilgrim land."[45]

The apostle Paul wrote: "Be imitators of me, as I am of Christ" (1 Cor 11:1). Believers of each age need holy ones—imitators of Christ—whom they themselves can imitate. Hopkins, in (*The Soldier*), portrays Christ as a soldier, who has experienced the hardships of war and fought to the end for the salvation of all. Hopkins, in the latter part of the poem, depicts Christ in heaven, looking down upon earth:

> There he bides in bliss
> Now, and seeing somewhere some man do all that man can do,
> For love he leans forth, needs his neck must fall on, kiss,
> And cry 'O Christ-done deed! So God-made-flesh does too:
> Were I come o'er again' cries Christ 'it should be this.'[46]

Jesus needs to make his presence and saving actions visible in human beings of each time and age; and, the poet Hopkins portrays him as leaning down from heaven and embracing and kissing a person he sees performing a "Christ-done deed," just as he himself would do it, should he come again. In the preceding pages I have offered examples of a number of persons who have tried, and, if still living, continue to strive to imitate Jesus the liberator.

Jesus the Liberator: A Dangerous Image

But the image of Jesus the liberator is one of the most provocative and "dangerous," if you will, of all the images of Jesus. And those who seek to imitate Jesus as liberator, in the public forum, are very often the subject of controversy and evoke strong feelings—positive and/or negative. Such is the case with Damien of Molokai, Dorothy Day, Rosemary Haughton, Oscar Romero, Pedro Cassadaliga and even Mother Teresa.

Damien was the subject of great controversy about his motivations, life-style, moral integrity and methods of dealing with the lepers of Molokai both during and after his death. Dorothy Day was an ardent pacifist, and her decision not to take sides in the civil war in Spain angered both Catholics, who saw the war as a crusade against communism, and liberals and radicals, who were passionately committed to the cause of the workers and peasants. As a biographer notes, "Dorothy's decision to take a neutral position in the war was a move guaranteed to provoke everyone's outrage."[47]

Rosemary Haughton's strong words about the oppression of women, even in the church, make her an object of controversy, even though she remains a faithful member of the church. Archbishop Oscar Romero, because he preached that violence could be used against an oppressive unjust regime, if every other measure was exhausted, is viewed by many people as a martyr, not for Christ, but for a political stance. Pedro Cassadaliga, because he has sided with certain revolutionary movements out of his sincere love for the poor, is viewed by many as too radical and political. Mother Teresa is criticized for limiting her work to caring for individuals and small groups, rather than seeking to bring about basic changes in institutions, which perpetuate the poverty and suffering of millions.

The followers of Jesus the liberator, whom I have described in this chapter, are all imperfect, sinful human beings. If they were all able to come together in a symposium on the meaning of Jesus the liberator, they would probably express some strong disagreements with each other. Ultimately, history and the people of God will decide how authentic these modern followers of Jesus the liberator really were. I have focused on these particular individuals because each of them reveals in his or her life and writings an intimate love of Jesus Christ and because they have expressed this love in a generative way, by dedicating themselves in their own unique ways to the service of the poorest of the poor.

Paul in his first letter to the Corinthians indicates that there are many charisms, distinct callings, within the people of God. I find it more helpful to look at the special gifts and the intensity of love, compassion, peace, hope, courage, joy that shine forth in the hearts of these little ones of God than to concentrate on the issues that divide them and the controversies that surround them. I leave these latter matters for discussion by others and to the judgment of history.

But all of us are called to ask ourselves if we are in love with Jesus as liberator of the poor and how we seek in our daily lives to liberate, as Jesus liberated. All of us are invited to put on the mind and the heart of Jesus the liberator, according to the inner inspirations of the Holy Spirit that arise deep within us. Archbishop

Romero said in a letter to his flock that it was a great joy for him to introduce himself as "a pastor who wants to live out, and, as closely as possible to share in, the feelings of the Good Shepherd who came not to be served but to serve, and to give his life" (Matt 20:28).[48] The apostle Paul said that we should seek to have the mind of Christ (Phil 2:5). If the deepest feelings of the heart reveal values to us, if they reveal Jesus the liberator to us and stir us to follow him, then we should also pray to have the "mind" and "feelings of Jesus," just as Archbishop Romero did. In this way we will ourselves become ardent imitators of Jesus the liberator, on fire with the inner fire that burned in Jesus' own heart, and eager to liberate from their misery the hungry, the thirsty, the stranger, the naked, the sick, all victims, wherever we encounter them.

Notes

1. Jaroslav Pelikan, *Jesus Through The Centuries* (New Haven: Yale University Press, 1985), p. 209.

2. Ibid., p. 218.

3. Vital Jourdain, *The Heart of Father Damien* (Milwaukee: Bruce Publishing Company, 1955), p. 231.

4. Ibid., p. 237.

5. Ibid., p. 243.

6. Dorothy Day, *The Long Loneliness* (New York: Harper and Brothers, 1952), p. 204.

7. Ibid., p. 205.

8. Ibid.

9. Dorothy Day, *From Union Square to Rome* (Silver Springs, Maryland: The Preservation of the Faith Press, 1938), p. 163.

10. Dorothy Day, *Loaves and Fishes* (New York: Harper and Row, 1963), p. 178.

11. Vital Jourdain, *The Heart of Father Damien*, p. 151.

12. Dorothy Day, *The Long Loneliness*, p. 285.

13. Cf. Victorio Araya, *God of the Poor* (Maryknoll, New York: Orbis Books, 1987), p. 58.

14. Cf. Leonardo Boff and Clodovis Boff, *Introducing Liberation Theology* (Maryknoll, New York: Orbis Books, 1987), p. 47.

15. Rosemary Haughton, *The Re-creation of Eve*, introduction by Nancy Schwoyer (Springfield, Illinois: Templegate Publishers, 1985), p. ii.

16. Ibid.

17. Cited by Robert Coles, *Dorothy Day: A Radical Devotion* (New York: Addison-Wesley Publishing Company, Inc., 1987), p. 75.

18. Cf. Rosemary Haughton, *The Re-creation of Eve*, pp. 52–54.

19. Cf. Elisabeth Schüssler Fiorenza, *In Memory of Her* (New York: Crossroad, 1984), p. 124.

20. Haughton, p. 14.

21. Ibid., p. 30.

22. Oscar Romero, *Voice of the Voiceless: The Four Pastoral Letters and Other Statements*, introductory essays by Jon Sobrino and Ignacio Martin-Baro (Maryknoll, New York: Orbis Books, 1985), p. 6.

23. Ibid., pp. 50–51.

24. Ibid., p. 51.

25. Ibid., p. 129.

26. Ibid., p. 71.

27. Ibid., p. 191.

28. Pedro Cassadaliga, *I Believe in Justice and Hope* (Notre Dame, Indiana: Fides/Claretian, 1978), p. 167.

29. Ibid.

30. Ibid., pp. 110–111.

31. Romero, p. 181.

32. Cassadaliga, pp. 213–214.

33. Ibid., p. 213.

34. Romero, p. 184.

35. Cassadaliga, p. 114.

36. Ibid., p. 215.

37. Ibid.

38. Ibid., p. 216.

39. Peter Milward, *A Commentary on the Sonnets of G.M. Hopkins* (Chicago: Loyola University Press, 1969), p. 102.

40. Romero, p. 184.

41. Cassadaliga, p. 225.

42. Ibid., p. 229.

43. Ibid., p. 225.

44. Ibid., p. 226.

45. Ibid., p. 225.

46. Peter Milward, p. 134.

47. Dorothy Day, *By Little and By Little: The Selected Writings of Dorothy Day*, edited and with an introduction by Robert Ellsberg (New York: Alfred A. Knopf, 1983), p. xxxi.

48. Romero, pp. 57–58.

4

First-Born of Many
Sisters and Brothers

Holy women and men throughout the centuries have found
great consolation and challenge in imaging Jesus as their brother.
Why? Is it worthwhile today for individuals to seek to cultivate
with the help of the Holy Spirit an affective response to Jesus as
brother? Will the nourishing of such a response lead to a deeper
love of all human beings as brothers and sisters? The beginnings of
an answer to these questions perhaps lie in reflections on how
Jesus dealt with those whom the New Testament describes as his
"brothers" and "sisters" by blood.

Jesus and His Kin

It is true that the Roman Catholic and some other Christian
churches believe, with support from some respected scripture
scholars, that those whom the New Testament describes as the
"brothers" and "sisters" of the Lord were not siblings, but rather
kin such as cousins. This issue is not critical here, however, because the basic family unit in Jesus' time was the extended family,
which included near relatives, and involved fierce loyalties. This
means that Jesus' relationships, even with cousins, would have a
quality of closeness that is not generally so present in contemporary families in the United States and various other countries as
well. It is then meaningful to reflect on Jesus' relationships with
his "brothers" and "sisters" in the flesh, even if the latter were not
siblings, but near relatives.

What kind of a brother was Jesus to his brothers and sisters by
blood? This is the type of question anyone might ask who experiences an invitation to discover in Jesus through faith a true
"brother" and to respond to him with sisterly or brotherly affection. But the answer to this question is not a simple one. There are

73

not many references in the gospels to the brothers and sisters of Jesus. And where Jesus is shown interacting with his brothers and sisters or speaking about them, the scene is generally one of tension rather than tender affection. Moreover, it is very difficult to get at what is historical in these accounts; consequently, I readily acknowledge the intuitive, conjectural character of my reflections on some of these texts. Still, it is worthwhile to raise the question about Jesus' relationship to his kin. For if the gospels do not ultimately portray Jesus as a man who truly loved his family, his brothers and sisters, then the believer might find herself or himself inclined to raise the objection: "If Jesus did not show real fraternal love for his own family, how can I respond from the heart to Jesus as brother with true sisterly or brotherly affection?"

"His Family Came To Take Charge of Him"

The relatives of Jesus make their first appearance in the gospel of Mark in a scene where they are trying to remove Jesus from a pressing crowd that was preventing him and his disciples from getting anything to eat. Mark says that "his family . . . came to take charge of him, saying, 'he is out of his mind' " (Mk 3:21 NAB). Matthew and Luke do not offer any account of this incident. Mark next recounts a seemingly harsh comment Jesus made when he was told that his mother and brothers were outside the place where he was meeting with his disciples and had sent word that they wanted him to come out. Instead of at once getting up and going out, Jesus turned to the crowd seated around him and said: " 'Who are my mother and my brothers?' And looking around on those who sat about him, he said, 'Here are my mother and my brothers! Whoever does the will of God is my brother and sister and mother' " (Mk 3:33–35). Luke in his account of this incident does not draw a contrast between Jesus' mother and brothers who are outside and his disciples who are within. Luke simply has Jesus say: "My mother and my brothers are those who hear the word of God and do it" (Lk 8:21).[1]

"Even His Brothers Did Not Believe in Him"

Mark, in his last reference to Jesus' kin, recalls an incident where Jesus returns home and teaches in the synagogue, but is rejected by the local listeners. The latter say: "Is not this the carpenter, the son of Mary and brother of James and Joses and Judas and Simon, and are not his sisters here with us?' " (Mk 6:3).

Jesus responds: "A prophet is not without honor, except in his own country, and among his own kin, and in his own house" (6:4). Matthew and Luke in recounting this saying of Jesus make no reference to Jesus' own kin, as Mark does, though they do tell of the violent reaction of townspeople to Jesus' teaching. Finally, the gospel of John describes an incident in which Jesus' brothers urge him to go up to Jerusalem and show himself to the world. Jesus refuses and John remarks that "even his brothers did not believe in him" (Jn 7:5).

Pentecostal Transformation of the Brothers of Jesus

If the gospel references to Jesus' brothers are charged with tension, doubt, struggle, and even opposition to Jesus, the references to the brothers of Jesus in the Acts of the Apostles and the epistles of Paul reflect the positive, faithful response of the brothers to the risen Jesus. Luke in the first chapter of Acts names the members of the small group of faithful gathered together after the ascension. He first mentions the apostles and then he adds: "All these with one accord devoted themselves to prayer, together with the women and Mary the mother of Jesus, and with his brothers" (Acts 1:14). Also, Paul in arguing for certain rights for himself and Barnabas writes: "Do we not have the right to eat and drink? Do we not have the right to marry a believing woman like the rest of the apostles and the brothers of the Lord and Cephas?" (1 Cor 9:4–5 NAB). Paul here provides evidence that the brothers of the Lord were among the disciples of the risen Lord. Indeed, in his letter to the Galatians Paul refers to his meeting in Jerusalem with "James, the brother of the Lord" (1:19) and he describes James as one of the "pillars" of the Jerusalem church (2:9). The references to the brothers of Jesus as faithful members of the early Christian community provide striking proof of the ultimate fruitfulness of Jesus' relationship with his brothers in the flesh.

The Extended Family in Jesus' Time

But what concretely do the gospel references to Jesus in his interactions with his brothers and sisters reveal to us about the kind of brother he was, about the kind of love he had for his sisters and brothers? Clearly, Jesus had a mission that called him beyond the confines of his own family and town. He had a vision that his relatives and even his mother found difficult to understand. Luke recounts that even as a twelve year old Jesus at least on one occasion was a source of deep anxiety and perplexity for his parents. On the way back from the celebration of the feast of the Passover in Jerusalem, Mary and Joseph discovered that Jesus was missing. When they finally found him in the temple after three days of frantic searching Mary quite understandably asked: "Son, why have you treated us so?" (Lk 2:48). Jesus replied: "Did you not know that I must be in my Father's house?" (2:49). Luke records that "they did not understand the saying which he spoke to them" (3:50). It is essential to understand Jesus' relationship to his kin, to his brothers and sisters, against the backdrop of the strong ties that bound families together in Jesus' time and his own uniqueness and calling. These factors provide a key to understanding why Jesus was the kind of brother he was to his sisters and brothers.

The family in Jesus' time was the fundamental unit of society and it included not just parents and their children, but relatives as well. Ties of blood and marriage were very strong. In fact,

> Not only were all members of the family regarded as brothers, sisters, mothers and fathers to one another but they identified themselves with one another. The harm done to one member of the family was felt by all.[2]

It is perhaps this intense solidarity of family members with one another that explains the incident Mark recounts where Jesus was hemmed in with his apostles by the crowds, "making it impossible for them to get any food whatever" and "his family heard of this [and] they came to take charge of him, saying, 'He is out of his mind'" (Mk 3:20–21 NAB). This incident may reflect both real concern of family members for Jesus' well-being and at the same time their complete incomprehension of his prophetic mission.

Jesus Announced the "Good News" to His Kin

Ironically, perhaps the greatest sign of Jesus' love for his family, his brothers and sisters is that they were among the first to whom he proclaimed the good news of the reign of God. Luke has Jesus teaching in the synagogue of Nazareth at the very beginning of his ministry (Lk 4:14–30). John shows Jesus working his first "sign" at a marriage feast in Cana in Galilee. Mary, the mother of Jesus, and his brothers are at the feast, and it is at the instigation of his mother that Jesus is led to turn the water into wine. In the incidents at the synagogue and the marriage feast we see Jesus praying with family members, celebrating a feast with them and, most importantly, sharing with them that which is closest to his heart: the good news that salvation is at hand. Certainly, it is difficult to sort out what is historical in these accounts; but the gospels in their totality make it very clear that Jesus did invite his kin to accept the good news. And what greater sign of love could he have shown to them—apart from his death on the cross?

Yet, though Jesus invited his kin to accept the gospel, there is no unambiguous evidence that any of his brothers or sisters responded positively to his offer until after his death and resurrection. Doubtless this must have caused Jesus much pain. There is no reason to think that Jesus did not feel the deep affection for family members that characterized families of his time. To presume the opposite would seem to fly in the face of everything else we know about Jesus as a deeply caring, compassionate, loving individual. It remains true that Jesus' prophetic activities and message proved a source of deep tension between him and his brothers and sisters, and this would have complicated affective exchanges between them. But in spite of these difficulties Jesus does seem to have remained in contact with family members, and at least some of these eventually did become converts after his death and resurrection.

Jesus' Unique Experience of the "Abba" and the Confusion of His Brothers

One of the greatest sources of friction between Jesus and his brothers and sisters may have been his recounting of his personal experience of God. For Jesus possessed an utterly unique sense of God as his Father. It is quite likely that Jesus himself said: "No one knows the Father except the Son and anyone to whom the Son chooses to reveal him" (Mt 11:27). Jesus expressed his deep sense of intimacy with his Father by addressing him as "abba." Children of Jesus' time used the word "abba" in speaking in an intimate, informal way with their fathers. A contemporary translation of "abba" might be "papa." When Orientals of Jesus' time called God Father, the word included something of what the word "mother" means for us today.[3] For this reason one scholar suggests that the word *imma* (mother) just "as readily captures the felt sense [of the divine reality Jesus calls 'abba']: *abba, imma,* our heavenly father and mother."[4] Jesus' brothers and sisters might well have asked: "Where did [our brother] get all this? What is the wisdom given to him?" (Mk 6:2).

Jesus' Conditions for "Kinship in the Kingdom"

Jesus' unique experience of God as "abba" led him to reveal God as "abba" to others. Jesus experienced God not only as intimately present to him, but as the compassionate, generous, forgiving, merciful One seeking to bring all into a new family, but especially the poor, the despised, the outcasts. In announcing the reign of God on earth, the institution of a new family of God's children, Jesus did not deny the value of blood ties. He urged the observance of the fourth commandment to honor one's father and one's mother. Indeed, Jesus' personal appreciation of the richness of family life probably inspired in part his use of family images to describe membership in the kingdom of God. At the same time Jesus found it necessary to utter some "hard sayings" about the limitations of human kinship in relationship to "kinship in the kingdom."

Jesus taught that kinship with him did not provide the key for entrance into the kingdom, but rather doing the will of God. When a woman cried out, "Blessed is the womb that bore you, and the breasts that you sucked!" (Lk 11:27), Jesus replied, "Blessed rather are those who hear the word of God and keep it.!" (Lk 11:28). Again, Jesus taught: "Call no man father on earth, for you have one Father, who is in heaven" (Mt 23:9), and "you have one teacher, and you are all [brothers and sisters]" (Mt 23:8). Even if Jesus is here referring to the use of professional titles the deeper implication is that obedience to God is primary and that all human commitments are to be measured in the light of commitment to God. Jesus taught in an uncompromising way that certain attachments to kin could even block entry into the kingdom of God. "If anyone comes to me and does not hate his own father and mother and wife and children and brothers and sisters . . . he cannot be my disciple" (Lk 14:26).

Jesus did not exclude his relatives from the kingdom, but, as with all others, he called them to undergo a conversion, to humble themselves, to enter into the kingdom of God and to accept as equals in the kingdom the poor, the outcasts, the tax collectors, the prostitutes. Jesus asked his brothers and sisters in the flesh to make a basic option, to choose for him and his message rather than against him. Jesus was speaking of the need to confront this option when he said that he had come not to bring peace, but a sword, "to set a man against his father, and a daughter against her mother" (Mt 10:34–35). Jesus called everyone to "face the sword of deciding," the "sword that divides the believer from the non-believer."[5] The fruit of a positive decision is entrance into a new family, the "kinship of the kingdom" in which all are equals as children of God and brothers and sisters of Jesus.

In sum, then, what kind of a brother was Jesus to his brothers and sisters by blood? He was a brother who loved his own family enough to invite them to share in the deepest secrets of his heart, to discover his beloved "abba" as their own "abba," to enter into the kingdom of the "abba." Jesus did not disavow his brothers and sisters in the flesh, but he asked them to look beyond the narrow confines of kinship and to become members of a new, universal family. The love of blood relatives for one another in this new family is not extinguished or diminished, but deepened. And everyone who enters into the new family of the kingdom of God acquires a whole multitude of new brothers and sisters as well.

Paul, Freud and Jesus' Title as "Elder Brother"

The apostle Paul in his epistle to the Romans depicts Jesus as the "eldest" (Rom 8:29) of many brothers and sisters. Sigmund Freud rather remarkably offers some succinct, highly perceptive observations about the Christian church that provide an excellent jump-off point for reflecting about Jesus as elder brother in the family of believers and about the response of believers to one another and to Jesus as brother. Freud remarks that Christ "stands to the individual members of the group of believers as a kind of elder brother."[6] He states that

> a democratic strand runs through the Church, for the very reason that before Christ everyone is equal, and that everyone has an equal share in his love. It is not without deep reason that the similarity between the Christian community and a family is involved, and that believers call themselves brothers in Christ, that is, brothers through the love which Christ has for them.[7]

Freud adds that "every Christian loves Christ as his ideal and feels united with all other Christians by the tie of identification."[8]

Equality of Women and Men as Sisters and Brothers of Jesus in the Kingdom

The New Testament most commonly refers to members of the family of the kingdom of God as "brothers." The word is used over one hundred and seventy times. The term is employed to designate both men and women, except in instances where a particular Christian woman is addressed. Paul, for example, at the conclusion of his epistle to the Romans writes: "I commend to you our sister Phoebe, a deaconess of the church at Cenchreae" (16:1). The predominant use of the male term "brothers" is not meant to imply an inequality between men and women as members of the kingdom, but it reflects the linguistic practice common until most recent times.

Here some basic questions spontaneously present themselves. What are the roots of the common New Testament custom of referring to believing Christians as "brother" or "sister"? Is this practice based on the way Jesus himself lived, taught and dealt with his followers? Did Jesus understand himself as a brother to his followers? Did he relate to his followers with true brotherly affection? Did he treat his male and female followers as equals to one another in the kingdom of God?

There is no doubt that the custom by which the first Christians referred to one another as brothers and sisters had its roots in the life and teaching of Jesus himself. Jesus possessed a deep affective experience of God as "abba" and of other human beings as children of his beloved "abba." Jesus constantly sought to reveal the "abba" to others as their beloved parent and to invite them to enter into the new family, the kingdom of the "abba." Jesus was a man of profound feelings, and his intense experience of God as "abba" to himself and others must have inspired in him the most tender brotherly feelings toward his followers. When Jesus turned to his followers and said that whoever did the will of God was his brother and sister, these words must have flowed not just from his mind but, above all, from the depths of his heart. And the love Jesus felt for his brothers and sisters was that of the older brother for his younger siblings because it was through him that the others were led to encounter God as "abba" and to enter into the kingdom.

Did Jesus view men and women as equals in the kingdom of the "abba"? Did he value his sisters in the kingdom as much as he valued his brothers? Jesus made it clear in many ways that *the* criterion for entering into the kingdom of God was doing the will of the "abba." He stressed that anyone who wished to enter the kingdom must "receive the kingdom of God like a child" (Mk 10:15) and that rank or social status meant nothing as far as membership in the kingdom is concerned. Even though Jesus chose twelve men as his apostles, when they got into an argument about who was the greatest he stated sharply and unequivocally that "whoever would be great among you must be your servant, and whoever would be first among you must be your slave" (Mt 20:26–27).

Is Jesus the Only Reliable Brother?

Jesus welcomed into his kingdom the destitute poor, the crippled and the sick, sinners, tax collectors, prostitutes.[9] In his parable about the laborers in the vineyard, where those hired last receive the same recompense as those who were hired first, Jesus "articulates the equality of all rooted in the gracious goodness of God."[10] "Jesus' parable thus startles his hearers into the recognition that God's gracious goodness establishes equality among all of us, righteous and sinner, rich and poor, men and women."[11] Jesus radiated the graciousness of the "abba." He loved his women-disciples as his own sisters and they, in turn, loved him as their brother, a brother who treated them as equals to their brothers in the kingdom.

One writer has recently asked: "Is God the Only Reliable Father?"[12] One might ask in similar terms: "Is Jesus the only unconditionally reliable brother?" There is a profound sense in which the answer to this question must be "yes." Jesus is the only male without sin (Heb 4:15). He alone among men has loved both men and women with the perfection of brotherly love. Jesus was with his brothers and sisters "as one who serves" (Lk 22:27) and as one who gave "his life as a ransom for many" (Mk 10:45). The most authentic brother is the one who does not lord it over his brothers or his sisters, but who values them as equal to one another in dignity and worth before God and who shows this respect in everything he does, even in dying. Jesus alone is the brother who sets all of his brothers and sisters free and enables them to become fully what they are called to be. Jesus is the only brother who fully and unconditionally exemplifies what a brother can be. Jesus is in this sense the only unconditionally reliable brother. Of course, the ultimate explanation of the perfect brotherhood of Jesus roots itself in his reality as unique Son of the "abba." As the "abba" says of Jesus, "This is my beloved Son: with thee I am well pleased"

(Mk 1:11), so each of us, whether brother or sister, can say to Jesus, "You are my beloved brother, in whom I delight without measure."

"Christ Rejoices That He Is Our Brother"

Julian of Norwich, the fourteenth century English mystic, recounts of one of her remarkable visions: "And so I saw that God rejoices that he is our Father and God rejoices that he is our Mother . . . and Christ rejoices that he is our brother." Julian includes Christ's joy that he is our brother among "five great joys" of God and she says that "these are five great joys . . . in which [God] wants us to rejoice."[13] But clearly we can only rejoice in Jesus as our brother to the extent that we possess an intimate knowledge and love of him precisely as our brother. What then are some further concrete ways through which we can come to a deeper appreciation and embrace of Jesus as our brother with our mind, heart, spirit? How can we more fully awaken those special sensitivities to value, those feelings of the heart that will disclose to us Jesus' reality as our brother in a richer, finer way than we have previously experienced?

Prefigurement of Jesus as Faithful Brother

Is it possible for us to learn about what Jesus means to us as our brother in a heartfelt way through reflecting not only on Jesus, but on the example of other brothers and sisters in our human family as well? One theologian tells us that "we cannot have an authentic understanding of humanity unless we first know Christ."[14] Christian belief most certainly affirms that Jesus Christ is the measure by which all brotherhood is to be measured. But holy scripture also reveals to us that the Spirit of Christ has been at work in human hearts from the very beginning of history. This means that we can find Jesus Christ as brother prefigured in the lives of brothers who lived before him and reflected in the lives of holy brothers and sisters who lived after him. It is appropriate to speak of Jesus our brother as reflected in the lives of both brothers and sisters because siblings of both genders share many common qualities.

The Jesuit poet Gerard Manley Hopkins was especially gifted with an exquisite awareness of how Christ is mirrored, how indeed he reveals himself in others. In his poem *As kingfishers catch fire* Hopkins tells us that "the just man"

> acts in God's eye what in God's eye he is—
> Christ—for Christ plays in ten thousand places,
> Lovely in limbs, and lovely in eyes not his
> To the Father through the features of men's faces.[15]

Again, as I noted earlier, in his sonnet (*The Soldier*) Hopkins portrays Christ as beholding from his bliss in heaven "some man do all that man can do"; Jesus is so moved that he leans forth from heaven, embraces and kisses the man and cries:

> 'O Christ-done deed! So God-made-flesh does too:
> Were I come o'er again . . . it should be this.'[16]

Finally, in his poem *Brothers* Hopkins portrays the tender affection that the older of two brothers shows for the younger at a performance the latter is giving in a school play. The poet begins with the words:

> How lovely the elder brother's
> Life all laced in the other's,
> Love-laced![17]

Hopkins was, of course, aware of the flaws that dim the image of Jesus as brother in us, but he ends his poem *Brothers* by acknowledging that despite the flaws there is a goodness that shines through us:

>   Ah Nature, framed in fault,
> There's comfort then, there's salt;
> Nature, bad, base, and blind,
> Dearly thou canst be kind;
> There dearly then, dearly,
> I'll cry thou canst be kind.[18]

We are indeed able to discover Christ as our brother reflected in the good and kind brothers and sisters of every age.

Abel and Jesus

The Hebrew Testament offers us stories of brothers who, at their best, foreshadow in their lives qualities Jesus our brother later embodies and, at their worst, reveal characteristics diametrically opposed to those we discover in Jesus. Abel, the first child of Adam, offers a sacrifice that God finds acceptable. Cain, the brother of Abel, out of jealousy and envy murders his brother. The gospels suggest a parallel between Jesus and Abel, who, though innocent, were murdered out of envy (cf. Mt 23:35; 27:18; Lk 11:47–54). John tells us in his first epistle that "we should love one another, and not be like Cain who was of the evil one and murdered his brother" (1 Jn 3:12). John adds that "anyone who hates his brother is a murderer . . . and . . . that no murderer has eternal life abiding in him" (3:15). John reminds us that "by this we know love, that he laid down his life for us; and we ought to lay down our lives for the brethren" (3:16). Here we see the radical contrast between Cain and Jesus. The former slays his brother out of envy and jealousy; the latter gives his life for his brothers and sisters out of love. Such is the character of our elder brother Jesus.

Joseph and His Brothers

The story of Joseph and his brothers also serves to shed light on the nature of true brotherhood and leads us to glimpse in Joseph a prefiguring of the tender love of Jesus our brother for us. In the Genesis account, Joseph, the beloved son of Jacob and Rachel, is sold by his brothers to some Egyptian slave traders because they envied the special love Jacob had for Joseph. Later Jacob sent his sons to Egypt to purchase grain during a famine. Joseph had become powerful in Egypt and he recognized his brothers, but did not reveal himself at that time. He insisted instead that they bring Benjamin, the youngest son of Jacob and Rachel, with them when they returned. They did; and after Joseph saw how great the love of the brothers was for Benjamin and their father, he revealed himself to them. He said: "I am your brother, Joseph, whom you sold into Egypt. And now do not be distressed or angry with yourselves, because you sold me here; for God sent me before you to preserve life" (Gen 45:5). Joseph told them also to make haste and bring his father Jacob and all his household to Egypt. "Then," Genesis recounts, Joseph "fell upon his brother Benjamin's neck and wept; and Benjamin wept upon his neck. And he kissed all his brothers and wept upon them" (45:14–15). Joseph is presented as an ideal brother, overflowing with generosity, love, forgiveness. Most certainly Joseph in his goodness and forgiveness foreshadows the marvelous, totally accepting love of Jesus, our older brother, for us.

Jesus in the parable of the "prodigal son" reflects the powerful affections we see in the story of Joseph and his brothers. But, most importantly, Jesus in the telling of the parable reveals his own heart to us. He shows us in the most moving fashion how he images his beloved "abba" and how he thinks an older brother should deal with a delinquent younger sibling, who returns, humbled and repentant, to his family home after a period of reckless living.

In the parable, the younger brother leaves his family, squanders his inheritance in loose living and returns when he has nowhere else to go. In language that echoes the words of the Joseph story in Genesis, Jesus says that when the younger son was yet at a distance "his father saw him and had compassion, and ran and embraced him and kissed him" (Lk 15:20). The father has the servants bring the best robe for his son, puts a ring on his finger and prepares a great feast. The older brother, who has always remained faithful to his father, hears the music and dancing, learns what has happened, is angry and refuses to go in. The father goes out to his older son, tells him how much he appreciates his faithfulness, but says that "it was fitting to make merry and be glad, for this your brother was dead, and is alive; he was lost, and is found" (15:32). Here we easily infer, from this parable Jesus himself told, how he, as our older brother, feels toward us as his delinquent siblings. He rejoices that we, his brothers and sisters, who were lost are now found, and he invites us to celebrate together with him, feasting, singing and dancing in the kingdom of the "abba." There is no room in the heart of our "eldest brother" for the resentment or envy we saw in Cain and the brothers of Joseph. Jesus is the compassionate, generous, merciful, forgiving brother who proves in all that he says and does and is that he is, indeed, the unique child of the always loving "abba."

The Seven Maccabees Brothers and their Mother

The biblical story of the Maccabees anticipates yet another dimension of the character of Jesus, our older brother. In the second book of Maccabees there is a story about a mother and her seven

sons who submitted to terrible tortures and finally death rather
than violate the precepts of their faith. We are told that "the
brothers and their mother encouraged one another to die nobly,
saying, 'The Lord God is watching over us and in truth has compassion on us' " (2 Mc 7:5–6). The mother and brothers continue
to encourage one another until only the youngest brother and the
mother are left. The mother tells her youngest son: "Do not fear
this butcher, but prove worthy of your brothers. Accept death, so
that in God's mercy I may get you back again with your brothers"
(7:29). The younger brother remains faithful, even though the
king falls into a rage and tortures him more than the others. "Last
of all, the mother dies, after her son" (7:41).

The example of the Maccabees brothers foreshadows the courage, love and fidelity of Jesus in laying down his life for us. Jesus
goes before us in submitting to suffering and death and empowers
all of us with the inner grace and strength of spirit necessary to
take up our cross and follow him. Moreover, like the mother of the
Maccabees, Mary, the mother of Jesus, stands faithfully with her
son until the end. And she becomes our mother through the gift of
her son (Jn 19:26–27), just as Jesus becomes the "first-born of
many brothers and sisters" through the gift of the "abba." Medita-
tion on the love of the Maccabees brothers for one another helps
us to comprehend in some manner the words with which Paul
concludes the eighth chapter to the Romans, a chapter in which he
a few lines earlier describes Jesus as "the first-born among many
brothers [and sisters]" (8:29):

> In all these things we are more than conquerors through him
> who loved us. For I am sure that neither death, nor life, nor
> angels, nor principalities, nor things present, nor things to
> come, nor powers, nor height, nor depth, nor anything else in
> all creation, will be able to separate us from the love of God in
> Christ Jesus our Lord (8:37–39.)

The love of our elder brother Jesus fills us with that hope, even in
the face of death, which the mother of the Maccabees expressed
when she told her youngest son: "Accept death, so that in God's
mercy I may get you back again with your brothers" (2 Mc 7:29).
Indeed, the resurrection of Jesus, our elder brother, confirms the
ultimate fruitfulness of the hope of the Maccabees brothers and
their mother and our hope as well.

Jesus Mirrored in His Spiritual Siblings

If reflecting on the lives of holy brothers who went before him can help us grow in our understanding of Jesus as brother, most certainly meditating on the lives of holy brothers and sisters who have followed after Jesus can enrich immeasurably our appreciation of Jesus as our eldest brother.

Each believer finds special delights at certain privileged moments in particular saints or persons of renowned holiness. This author is presently drawn by bonds of affection to reflect briefly on Bernard of Clairvaux, Thérèse of Lisieux, and Charles de Foucauld as persons who in unique ways move the heart to love Jesus as brother and to love others as sisters and brothers of Jesus. It is only possible to focus on one or two incidents in the lives of these holy ones of God as a means of deepening, above all, the feelings of the heart in its response to Jesus as brother and to others as the little brothers and sisters of Jesus. Each reader is also invited to explore the particular attractions of the heart that draw her or him toward specific holy persons and to engage in meditative reflections similar to the ones that occupy us now.

Bernard of Clairvaux and His Brother Gerard

Saint Bernard of Clairvaux (1090–1153) was a highly gifted individual with many talents. He was a monastic reformer and a mystic. He could inspire individuals to do great things. In fact, when he entered the monastery at a young age he brought twenty-nine others with him, including four out of his five brothers. His youngest brother soon followed. What I want briefly to dwell on here is Bernard's reflections on the death of one of his brothers. It tells us much about brotherly love and offers indirect intimations of what the love of Jesus our brother must be for us.

Bernard's lament at the death of his brother Gerard is a passionate testimony to the strength and intimacy of a brother's love for a brother. Bernard, abbot of Clairvaux at the time of Gerard's death, was presenting a commentary to his brother monks on the Song of Songs. But his grief was so intense that it impelled him to insert into his commentary an account of the piercing sorrow he was experiencing and his attempt to deal with it as brother and believer. Bernard's reflections on his brother's concern for him, even though Gerard is now in heaven, provide intimations of what the love of the risen Jesus, as our brother, is for each one of us.

"Who Ever Loved Me As He?"

Bernard initially asks in anguish: "Who ever loved me as he? My brother by blood, but bound to me more intimately by religious profession [i.e. as a brother-monk]."[19] He acknowledges that the fact that Gerard was his blood brother "certainly mattered" but he says that "our spiritual affinity, our similar outlooks and harmony of temperaments, drew us more close still."[20] Bernard shows himself to be all too human in expressing such diverse emotions as resentment, anger, sadness, helplessness as he reflects on the terrible vacuum his brother's death has created in his life. In his pain he cries out: "Oh if I could only die at once and follow you."[21] In words tinged with a certain spontaneous resentment Bernard remarks: "What a harvest of joys, what a profusion of blessings is yours. Instead of my insignificant person you have the abiding presence of Christ."[22]

"You Will Not Forget Me Forever"

In his loneliness Bernard says to his brother: "How I long to know what you think of me, once so uniquely yours."[23] The idea flashes through Bernard's mind that his brother "no longer has the power to experience or relish anything but God, and what God himself experiences and relishes, because he is filled with God."[24] But this reflection terminates in a deeper insight and a renewed hope: "God is love, and the deeper one's union with God, the more full one is of love. And though God cannot endure pain, he is not without compassion for those who do; it is his nature to show mercy and pardon."[25] This means, Bernard says to his brother, that "you too must of necessity be merciful, clasped as you are to him who is Mercy."[26] Indeed, "your love has not been diminished but only changed; when you were clothed with God you did not divest yourself of concern for us, for God is certainly concerned about us." This realization renews a spirit of consolation and deep affection in Bernard. He says to his brother: "All that smacks of weakness you have cast away, but not what pertains to love. And since love never comes to an end, you will not forget me forever."[27] Bernard turns to his fellow monks and says: "It seems to me that I can almost hear my brother saying: Can a woman forget the son of her womb? And if she should forget, yet I will not forget you."[28]

Bernard's love for Gerard shows us what a powerful bonding factor the tie of blood is. But Bernard, like Jesus, acknowledges that spiritual bonding and affinity is richer, deeper, more intimate than mere physical relationship. Bernard desires to be with his brother, since he realizes that his brother is with Jesus in paradise and has by far the better lot. Bernard understands that his brother most certainly cares for him, even in bliss, because Gerard shares in God's love, and the love of God is a compassionate, merciful, attentive love. But if Bernard is correct that his brother Gerard cares for him, Gerard's care is but a dim reflection of the compassionate brotherly love Jesus has for each one of us, even in his bliss. Nor is it a pious exaggeration to say that Jesus cares for us with a brotherly love, because Jesus himself, in his earthly ministry, viewed his disciples with love as his brothers and sisters. We can then in the reflections of Bernard on the death of his brother Gerard learn not only how beautiful, strong, and yet tender—it has the tenderness of a mother's love—a brother's love for a brother is, but we are also graced with a glimpse of the gentle, kind, compassionate brotherly love Jesus, as our elder brother, has for each of us.

Thérèse of Lisieux and Her "Brothers"

Now what, one might spontaneously ask, does Bernard of Clairvaux have in common with Saint Thérèse of Lisieux? And how can the latter, who had no brothers, teach us about brotherly love? Thérèse did, in fact, have brothers, but they did not survive. Thérèse did have four sisters; and, like the brothers of Bernard, all of Thérèse sisters eventually entered the same religious order.

Thérèse lived at a time when there was no thought about the possibility of women priests. Yet she did tell others how much she would have loved to be a priest, and what she would have done as a priest.[29] On the day of her profession as a Carmelite sister, she prayed that since she was not able to be a priest "she wanted a priest to receive in her place the Lord's graces, to have the same aspirations, the same desires as she."[30] Toward the end of her life the prayer was answered. Near the conclusion of her *Story of a Soul* she writes: "For a very long time, I had a desire which appeared totally unrealizable to me, that of having *a brother as a priest* [emphasis that of Thérèse]. I often thought that had my little brothers not flown away to heaven, I would have had the happiness of seeing them mount the altar; but since God chose to make little angels of them, I could not hope to see my dream realized. And yet, not only did Jesus grant me the favor I desired, but he united me in the bonds of the spirit to two apostles, who became my brothers."[31] Our focus here is on the younger of the two "brothers."

Confidant and Consoler

Thérèse mentions the day that her superior told her that there was a young seminarian who requested that a sister pray for him so that after he was ordained he might be a good missionary. He in turn promised to "remember the one who would become his sister at the Holy Sacrifice each day after he was ordained."[32] His name was Maurice Belliere. Thérèse joyously writes: "My desire [for a brother as a priest] answered in this unexpected way, gave birth in my heart to a joy which I can describe only as that of a child. I would really have to go back to my childhood days to recapture once more the memory of joys so great that the soul is too little to contain them, and not for years had I experienced this kind of happiness." She adds that "I felt my soul was renewed; it was as if someone had struck for the first time musical strings left forgotten until then."[33]

Thérèse writes letters to her "little brother" glowing with warmth. Indeed, Thérèse writes with the same sense of intimacy she would use in writing to a blood relative. In response to a letter of Maurice she says : "O my dear little Brother, please never think you 'bore me or distract me', by speaking much about yourself."[34] "Would it be possible," she says, "for a sister not to take an interest *in all* that touches her brother?"[35] In response to yet another letter Thérèse remarks: "From your letter of the 14th my heart thrilled tenderly as I understood more than ever the degree to which your soul is sister to mine, since it is called to lift itself to God by the *elevator* of love and not to climb the rough staircase of fear."[36]

In one letter Maurice inquired rather discreetly about Thérèse's real name; but he apologized for perhaps intruding on her privacy as a Carmelite sister. Thérèse, in reply, tells him not only her name, but also details about her family life and the story of her entry into the Carmelites. She tells him that she wants him to be simple both with God and with her because she is, after all, his *sister.*[37] Not realizing the seriousness of her illness, Maurice asked Thérèse if she would write to him more often during his vacation, since her letters helped him so much. Thérèse replied that ". . . the Spouse is at the door" and that she would "scrawl more little notes" if God prolonged her pilgrimage. But she added: ". . . most probably I shall be doing better than writing to my dear little Brother . . . I shall be very *near* him, I shall see all he needs, and I shall give the good God no rest till He has given me all I want!"[38] Thérèse was enduring great physical suffering and inner spiritual darkness at this time, yet her letter seeks to refresh and encourage her "little brother" in his faith and hope."

"As a Stallion Stalwart, Very Violet Sweet"

The words of Thérèse may at times seem almost too sweet, too soft, like the face of a tiny violet on a mountainside; but they come from a heart as strong and lasting as the mountain itself. The poet Hopkins in his rapturous *Hurrahing in Harvest* sings of Jesus:

And the azurous hung hills are his world-wielding shoulder
Majestic—as a stallion stalwart, very-violet-sweet![39]

Thérèse, like Jesus, is also at once "very-violet-sweet" and yet "stalwart" at her heart's core.

Thérèse in her sisterly love for her "little brother" shows that the bonds of spiritual kinship can be as strong, as deep, as tender as any bonding to another by blood. Indeed, Thérèse shows that kinship in Christ can actually release the deepest forces of natural affection within a person. But at the same time the spiritual kinship of brothers and sisters in Christ opens them up to a hope and love that goes beyond the frontiers and capacities of mere human loving or physical kinship. Thérèse in telling Maurice of her realization of the degree to which his soul was sister to her own also reveals how a sister, as well as a brother in Christ, can flash forth and image Jesus, the elder brother.

There are many qualities that sisters and brothers as siblings have in common. We can often recognize the qualities of sisters in their brothers and of brothers in their sisters. These qualities can be superficial—a similarity in laugh—or they can be as deep as the heart itself. In the case of Thérèse, she mirrored in her tender, confident, prayers for her little sisters and brothers the deepest longings of the heart of Jesus, who lives to intercede for us. Thérèse loved Jesus most intimately, but her love did not turn inward but outward. It was a generous, fruitful love, filled with God's own compassion. Like Bernard's brother Gerard, Thérèse too in the bliss of heaven continues to turn eyes of compassion toward all the little sisters and brothers of Jesus here on earth. For every authentic love of Jesus is a generative love, a love that bears fruit in abundance.

Charles de Foucauld

Charles de Foucauld (1858–1916), unlike Bernard and Thérèse, who entered into monastic life quite young, led a rather turbulent, dissipated life in his early years. He lost his faith during his secondary studies. He was discharged from the army because of his dissolute living: he brought his mistress along to each place he was posted. But during a period of scholarly research in the Sahara he underwent a profound religious conversion. He was twenty-eight at the time. Initially, he joined the Trappists. But the life of a hermit attracted him still more. He lived in Nazareth as a hermit for three years. He was ordained a priest in 1901 and returned to the Sahara to establish a hermitage at Beni-Abbes on the Moracco-Algerian frontier. He lived a life of prayer and austerity. He sought to make converts to Christianity from the Moslem desert tribes, not by preaching but by good example. He had no disciples during his life and was murdered by a maurading band of fanatics in 1916.

Charles in his writings indicated a plan to found two religious congregations that he wished to call respectively The Little Brothers of Jesus and The Little Sisters of Jesus. He did not live to see his dream realized, but in 1933 Rene Voillaume founded The Little Brothers of Jesus and in 1939 Sister Madeleine of Jesus established the congregation of The Little Sisters of Jesus. Both drew their inspiration from the life and writings of Charles de Foucauld.

"Embraced, Like a Little Boy, by My Older Brother Jesus"

During a retreat Charles made in 1902 he wrote with deep affection: "I am in the house at Nazareth, between Mary and Joseph, embraced, like a little boy, by my elder brother Jesus."[40] Rene Voillaume writes of Charles' "constant intimacy with his 'beloved Brother and Lord Jesus', as he was fond of calling him with an infinite reverence blended with great tenderness."[41] The rich affective relationship Charles enjoyed with Jesus shines out in the following words he jotted down: "When you are sad, tired, lonely and full of suffering, take refuge in the sanctuary of your soul and there you will find your Brother . . . Jesus, who will console you, support you and strengthen you."[42] Charles' loving relationship with Jesus as his older brother remained a constant in his life, since in 1916, the year of his death, he wrote: "Jesus is our elder brother. Let us live, think, speak and act as the younger brothers of Jesus."[43] Obviously Charles was given a very special charism of appreciation of Jesus as older brother.

But the intimacy Charles experienced with Jesus as his older brother was a generative intimacy, an intimacy that bore fruit in humble service and availability to others. Even though Charles lived a profoundly contemplative life in his hermitage, one scholar reminds us that "prayer did not keep him [Charles] apart from his fellow-men. He allowed himself to be interrupted, sent no one away, kept no one waiting."[44] In fact, a desert tribesman who knew him exclaimed in amazement: "He never kept us waiting."[45] And Charles exhorted himself in his journal to "be kind and compassionate"; to "let no distress leave you unmoved"; to "spend your life in the love of your neighbor."[46]

"Universal Brother"

Rene Voillaume in an exhortation he gave to members of the congregation of The Little Brothers of Jesus remarked that "if Father de Foucauld chose the name 'Little Brothers of Jesus' for his disciples to come, it was not just because he was fond of it as a term, but because it seemed to him so aptly to express the ideal that had formed itself in his mind and heart."[47] For Charles, intimacy with Jesus our brother necessarily turns us into brothers and sisters of all, universal brothers and sisters. Pope Paul VI in his encyclical *Populorum Progressio* says that the charity of Charles de Foucauld earned for him the title "Universal Brother."[48]

Charles de Foucauld as "Universal Brother" reflects Jesus who alone is truly "Universal Brother" in the deepest sense of the word. Jesus in his parable of the good Samaritan teaches that each of us is called to be a "universal neighbor" in befriending anyone in need. Charles was reflecting Jesus' teaching when he said, "Let no distress leave you unmoved." In scripture there is a difference in the narrow sense between "neighbor" and "brother." As one scholar observes: "Unlike a brother, to whom a man is bound by a natural relationship, the neighbor does not belong to the father's house"; thus, "if my brother is another I, my neighbor is other than I, another who can remain for me an 'outsider'; but the

neighbor "can also become a brother [or sister]."[49] Jesus teaches
that we are called to be universal neighbors, brothers and sisters,
because we are called to minister to anyone in need. And he tells
us that as often as we offered some service, e.g. feeding the
hungry, clothing the naked, visiting a prisoner, "to one of the least
of these my brethren, you did it to me" (Mt 25:40).

Today there exist The Little Brothers of Jesus and The Little
Sisters of Jesus who live lives of prayer, manual labor and austerity
in the service of the very least among us. These are all the brothers
and sisters of Charles, who now has reaped a hundredfold of good
things in heaven and a host of brothers and sisters here on earth
(Mk 10:30). And what are the roots of this fruitfulness? Certainly
there are many elements in the life of Charles that contribute to
his ongoing apostolic fecundity. But Charles' special love of Jesus
as older brother is a central source of the continuing stream of gifts
he bestows upon us. Charles had a unique experience in prayer of
the embrace of Jesus, his older brother, and in his last days he
exhorts his followers to come: "Let us live, think, speak and act as
the younger brothers of Jesus." We are reminded again of the poet
Hopkins' lines: "How lovely the elder brother's life all laced in the
other's-love laced." In Charles de Foucauld we see a shining example of the truth that authentic intimacy with Jesus blossoms into
universal love, charity toward all.

It is appropriate to conclude our reflections on Jesus as brother
with a few questions. What have I been like as a brother or sister to
my own siblings? What am I like now? What kind of a brother or
sister to my own siblings would I like to be in the future? Do I view
all afflicted persons as my brothers and sisters with whom Christ
identifies himself? Do I see a real value in praying for the gift of
experiencing truly fraternal or sisterly affections toward Jesus? Do
I sense the value and importance of meditating on the lives of holy
individuals, who each, in his or her own way, reveals Christ to us as
our brother? Finally, do I learn what it means to be a true brother
and sister from Jesus Christ or do I learn from my many human
"brothers" and "sisters" what Jesus really means as brother?
Or, as Hopkins asked in another context, "O which one? is it
each one?"[50]

Notes

1. Cf. Raymond E. Brown, *Biblical Exegesis and Church Doctrine* (New
York: Paulist Press, 1985), pp. 93–94.

2. Albert Nolan, *Jesus Before Christianity* (New York: Orbis Books, etc. 1978), p. 59.

3. Joachim Jeremias, *The Prayers of Jesus,* Studies in Biblical Theology, Second Series, 6 (Naperville, Ill: Alec R. Allenson, 1967), p. 95.

4. Donald Goergen, O.P., *The Mission and Ministry of Jesus* (Wilmington, Delaware: Michael Glazier, 1987), p. 143.

5. Raymond E. Brown, *Biblical Exegesis and Church Doctrine,* p. 93.

6. Sigmund Freud, *Group Psychology and the Analysis of the Ego,* translated by James Strachey (New York: Norton, 1975), p. 66.

7. Ibid.

8. Ibid.

9. Elisabeth Schüssler Fiorenza, *In Memory of Her* (New York: Crossroad, 1984), p. 122.

10. Ibid., p. 131.

11. Ibid., p. 132.

12. Diane Tennis, *Is God the Only Reliable Father?* (Philadelphia: Westminster Press, 1985).

13. Julian of Norwich, *Julian of Norwich—Showings,* translated and introduced by Edmund Colledge, O.S.A. and James Walsh, S.J. (New York: Paulist Press, 1978), p. 279.

14. Jerome Murphy-O'Connor, *Becoming Human Together* (Wilmington, Delaware: Michael Glazier, Inc., 1982), p. 36.

15. Peter Milward, S.J., *A Commentary on the Sonnets of G.M. Hopkins* (Chicago: Loyola University Press, 1969), p. 114.

16. Ibid., p. 134.

17. Gerard Manley Hopkins, *Gerard Manley Hopkins* (Baltimore: Penguin Books, 1958), p. 48.

18. Ibid.

19. Bernard of Clairvaux, *The Works of Bernard of Clairvaux: On the Song of Songs II,* trans., by Kilian Walsh; introduction by Jean Leclercq (Kalamazoo: Cistercian Publications, 1976), p. 61.

20. Ibid., p. 68.

21. Ibid., p. 67.

22. Ibid., p. 63.

23. Ibid.

24. Ibid.

25. Ibid.

26. Ibid.

27. Ibid.

28. Ibid.

29. Patricia O'Connor, *In Search of Therese* (Wilmington, Delaware: Michael Glazier, 1987), p. 125.

30. Ibid., p. 126.

31. Therese of Lisieux, *The Autobiography of St. Therese of Lisieux,* a new translation from the original manuscripts by John Clarke, O.C.D. (Washington D.C.: I.C.S. Publications, 1976), p. 250.

32. Ibid., p. 251.

33. Ibid.

34. Ibid., p. 134.

35. Ibid.

36. Ibid., p. 135.

37. Ibid., p. 137.

38. Ibid., p. 135.

39. Gerard Manley Hopkins, *A Commentary on the Sonnets of Hopkins,* p. 48.

40. Charles de Foucauld, *Meditations of a Hermit: The Spiritual Writings of Charles de Foucauld,* translated from the French by Charlotte Balfour (New York: Benziger Brothers, 1930), pp. 160–161.

41. Rene Voillaume, *Seeds of the Desert* (Notre Dame, Indiana: Fides Publishers, 1964), p. 23.

42. Charles de Foucauld, *Meditations of a Hermit: The Spiritual Writings of Charles de Foucauld,* p. 132.

43. Charles de Foucauld, *Spiritual Autobiography of Charles de Foucauld,* translated from the French by J. Holland Smith (New York: P.J. Kennedy and Sons), p. 197.

44. Elizabeth Hamilton, *The Desert My Dwelling Place* (London: Hodder and Staughton, 1968), p. 242.

45. Ibid.

46. Ibid.

47. Rene Voillaume, *Seeds of the Desert* (Chicago: Fides Publishers, 1955), p. 93. Please note that there are different editions of *Seeds of the Desert* and that they differ somewhat in content.

48. Cf. Elizabeth Hamilton, *The Desert My Dwelling Place,* p. 215.

49. Xavier Leon-Dufour, *Dictionary of Biblical Theology,* article on "Neighbor" (New York: Seabury Press, 1973), p. 385.

50. Gerard Manley Hopkins, *Gerard Manley Hopkins,* p. 61.

5

Wisdom-Friend
of the Gospels

Nothing so enriches and delights the human heart as friendship. Even marriage, the most intimate of human relationships, proves disappointingly shallow, unfulfilling, if the spouses are not best or, at the very least, close friends to one another. The words of Sirach ring as true today as they did two thousand years ago: "There is nothing so precious as a faithful friend" (6:15).

"God Is Friendship"

To the Christian believer Jesus reveals himself as friend and living presence within friendships. The monk Aelred of Rievaulx dared to "translate" John's great affirmation, "God is love" (1 Jn 4:16), as "God is friendship."[1] The Christian believes that God is Abba, Word and Spirit and that "the three Persons are the perfect community, not two in one flesh, but three subjects of a single, dynamic . . . consciousness."[2] The three Persons dwell within one another in an infinitely rapturous, joyous, communion of knowing and loving. If, then, Jesus is the Word made flesh, who calls us to share in his own friendship with the Abba and the Spirit, he is indeed our friend in a unique and most intimate fashion. Jesus also abides as an indwelling presence in our friendships with one another, since we have communion with one another through him and in him.

Jesus empowers us through his Holy Spirit to confess from the depths of our hearts: We believe in God, who is friendship. We believe that through Jesus we become friends of God. We believe in the "communion of friends." We believe that through Jesus we are introduced into the "communion of saints," which is the communion of the friends of God with one another. We believe in the resurrection from the dead. We believe that in the world to come "we shall always be with the Lord" (1 Thes 4:17) and with one another in an eternal communion of friendship.

Holy scripture is the fountainhead of all reflections on Jesus as friend. The lives and testimonies of the saints provide another privileged source of knowledge about the "lived reality" of friendship with Jesus. My reflection on Jesus as friend begins then in the present chapter with holy scripture and unfolds in the next two chapters to embrace the experiences of the saints. But the saints too constantly quench their thirst for deeper affective knowledge of Jesus as friend by drinking at the wellspring of holy scripture and of the sacraments. I will mirror this "return to the sources" on the part of the saints in my own meditations on the saints in their friendships with Jesus and with one another in Jesus.

Rabbi Jesus

How did Jesus meet the individuals who became his friends? The title the gospels most frequently give to Jesus is "teacher." Pelikan tells us that it seems safe to say that it was as "rabbi Jesus" that Jesus "was known and addressed by his immediate followers and others."[3] Pelikan also suggests that Jesus' innovative sayings and the authority with which he taught gradually led his followers to view him as a teacher-prophet.[4] In later ages Christian believers preferred to focus on the more exalted titles of Jesus. But it was as "rabbi" that Jesus first encountered those who became his disciples and followers. It was then in his role as teacher that Jesus most likely met those who were to become his most intimate friends. It is for this reason that I refer to Jesus as Wisdom-Friend.

Wisdom and Her Children

In teaching Jesus commonly used proverbs, parables, beatitudes. These were the typical forms of expression that the wisdom-teachers of Israel had used. Jesus' invitations and promises also at times echo and deepen those of the sages of Israel. In Sirach Wisdom cries out: "Come to me, you who desire me" (24:19). In Matthew Jesus says: "Come to me, all who labor and are heavy laden, and I will give you rest" (11:28). Again, in Proverbs Wisdom exclaims: "Come, eat of my bread and drink of the wine I have mixed . . . and live and walk in the way of insight" (9:5–6). Jesus proclaims: "Learn from me; for I am gentle and lowly in heart, and you will find rest for your souls" (Mt 11:29). Jesus reveals himself as Wisdom-teacher and as one who delights in inviting others to learn from him and share in the gifts of rest and peace which he offers.

Chief among those to whom Jesus extends his invitations and makes his promises are "the impoverished, starving, and 'heavy laden' countrypeople," the "tax collectors, sinners, women, children, fishers, housewives."[5] Because Jesus offers the "bread" and "wine" of his wisdom to outcasts with whom he eats and drinks his enemies say of him: "Behold, a glutton and a drunkard, a friend of tax collectors and sinners!" (Mt 11:19). In response to the accusation of his enemies Jesus replies: "Wisdom is justified by all her children" (Lk 7:35). Elisabeth Schüssler Fiorenza suggests that through his enigmatic statement about Wisdom and her children Jesus wished to indicate that *all* the children of Israel are children of Wisdom. She also suggests that Jesus probably understood himself as "prophet and child" of the God who is Wisdom.[6] Jesus' enemies were indeed correct when they called him a friend of tax collectors and sinners. For Jesus, as Wisdom-teacher, delighted to share his message of good news and his company with the little ones, and it was from this group that most of his closest followers and friends came.

Qualities of the Friendships of Jesus

The New Testament does not provide us with a treatise on friendship nor does it tell us in any detail how Jesus the teacher gradually became Jesus the friend to certain persons. Yet the gospels do provide some descriptions of Jesus in his initial encounters with persons who were destined to become his close friends; they also depict Jesus concretely interacting with persons whom he had come to know as close friends. Finally, the gospels place on the lips of Jesus certain sayings about friendship. These scriptural accounts root themselves in the life and words of the Jesus of history; but they also represent creative reflections on the deeds and teachings of Jesus by believers in the post-resurrection period. My aim here is not to arrive at a sharp distinction between the actual events and sayings of Jesus and later creative reflections of the evangelists about Jesus, but simply to provide a sketch of key features of Jesus' relationships with his friends and his views on friendship as the gospels present them. Also, my own reflections inevitably involve a subjective and hypothetical element, since they depend upon the scholars I have read, the religious experiences I have had, and a certain exercise of creative imagination.

Initiative, Mutual Attraction, Freedom

Friendships begin in an encounter. Mark, in the first chapter of his gospel, tells us that Jesus saw Simon and Andrew fishing and that he at once called them to follow him. And they did. Jesus then strolled a bit farther, saw James and John mending their fishing nets, invited them to follow him, and they too went with him at once. John in the first chapter of his gospel depicts John the Baptist as pointing out Jesus to two of his disciples. The two immediately start to follow Jesus. At this point John recounts: "Jesus turned and saw them following, and said to them, 'What do you seek?' And they said to him, 'Rabbi' (which means Teacher), 'where are you staying?' He said to them, 'Come and see.' They came and saw where he was staying; and they stayed with him that day" (Jn 1:38–39). One of these two was Andrew and the other perhaps John himself. The next day Andrew invited his brother Peter to meet Jesus. Peter too at once followed Jesus. The differences in the accounts of Mark and John are not pertinent for us here. What is important is what these accounts suggest to us about the initial stage of Jesus' friendships with Andrew, Peter, James and John.

The friendships of Jesus with his first disciples begin with a mutual attraction and a free decision on the part of each one to enter into a relationship. However, even in John, it is really Jesus who is the primary initiator of the relationships, since he at once asks Andrew and John what they are seeking and then invites them to come and see where he dwells. Jesus is portrayed as teacher in John, and the relationships, which will culminate in deep friendship, begin as those of students attracted to the unique rabbi, Jesus of Nazareth. Clearly the impact of the initial encounter of Andrew and John with Jesus is profound, since they "stayed with him that day" and Andrew could hardly wait to introduce his brother Simon to Jesus. The gospel verses we have just read suggest then that the initial marks of friendship with Jesus are mutual attraction, freedom, spending time together and talking about matters of common interest.

It is important to keep in mind as we imaginatively reflect on the origin, developments and qualities of the friendships of Jesus that everything in the gospels is written for us and our salvation. This means that when we read such words of Jesus as "What do you seek?" and "Come and see," we should image in our hearts Jesus speaking these words to us and what kind of response we find ourselves drawn to make. Then the words of the first epistle of Peter will become an ever more accurate description of our own inner state of mind and heart: "Without having seen him you love him; though you do not now see him you believe in him and rejoice with unutterable and exalted joy" (1 Pet 1:8).

Intimate Communication

Friendships grow according to the quality and depth of communication between friends. At the last supper Jesus said to the eleven close friends gathered around him at table: "I have called you friends, for all that I have heard from my Father I have made known to you" (Jn 15:15). Jesus' apostles certainly formed the nucleus of the group of little ones about whom he spoke in his hymn of jubilation: "I thank thee, Father . . . that thou hast hidden these things from the wise and understanding and revealed them to babes" (Mt 11:25). And what Jesus revealed to these little ones was not abstract truths, but the deepest personal knowledge of his heart. "All things have been delivered to me by my Father, and no one knows the Son except the Father, and no one knows the Father except the Son and any one to whom the Son chooses to reveal him" (Mt 11:27). The greatest proof of Jesus' deep friendship with his apostles was his intimate communication with them about his beloved Abba and the mystery of his own unique relationship as Son to the Abba. Jesus' revelation of this deepest mystery of his heart to his apostles not only emboldened them to call God "Abba," but it also inspired them to call Jesus "Friend."

Delight in Each Other's Presence

Close friends not only wish good for each other, but they delight in each other's presence. Jesus clearly enjoyed deeply his friendship with Mary and Martha and their brother Lazarus. In the words of the beloved disciple, "Jesus loved Martha and her sister and Lazarus" (Jn 11:5), and this delighting love was mutual. Shortly after John recounts Jesus' raising of Lazarus from the dead, he tells us of a supper that Lazarus and his sisters gave for Jesus at Bethany. At the dinner Mary "took a pound of costly ointment of pure nard and anointed the feet of Jesus and wiped his feet with her hair; and the house was filled with the fragrance of the oint-

ment" (Jn 12:3). Whatever deeper symbolism this anointing may
have had, it stands out in its basic simplicity as an act of tender,
appreciative, delighting love. Elsewhere in the gospels Mary is
shown sitting at Jesus' feet, listening to his teaching. Here we see
Jesus, the teacher, sharing his wisdom with Mary, the disciple,
who sits in rapt attention. This is perhaps the first encounter of
Mary with Jesus, the Wisdom-teacher, who was to become Mary's
Wisdom-friend. Jesus tells Martha, who complains that Mary had
left her to do all the serving: "Mary has chosen the good portion,
which shall not be taken away from her" (Lk 10:42). On the occasion of the anointing at Bethany and in this latter encounter of
Jesus with Mary, complaints are made about Mary's actions, which
totally focus on Jesus in apparent disregard of all else. In each
instance Jesus defends Mary's actions and reveals his delight in
Mary and her attention. Mutual delight in each other's presence is
characteristic of the encounters of Jesus and Mary.

Rejoicing and Sorrowing Together

Friends invite close friends to share in their most privileged
joys, and they seek consolation from these same friends in moments of deepest sorrow. C.F.D. Moule suggests that already during his public ministry Jesus perhaps "had a 'numinous' presence
which was occasionally recognized."[7] Yet Jesus chose Peter,
James and John, three of his closest apostle-friends, to share in a
unique manifestation of his numinous presence and glory. "He led
them up on a high mountain apart. And he was transfigured before
them, and his face shone like the sun, and his garments became
white as light" (Mt 17:1–2). Peter, in his ecstasy, said to Jesus:
"Lord, it is well that we are here" (Mt 17:4). Peter, if he could,
would remain there in the presence of the beauty and radiance of
Jesus. As Simone Weil says: "Beauty is that which we cannot wish
to change. . . . We simply desire that it should be."[8] But the
moment of "transfiguration" passed, and when the three apostles
looked up "they saw no one but Jesus only" (Mt 17:8). It would
not be long before this same Jesus would lead Peter, James and
John deep into the garden of Gethsemane and, in acute distress
and agony, beg them to stay and watch with him (Mk 14:34). This
time, however, Peter would not remain attentive to his Lord; instead he would fall asleep. Peter found it very easy to be with Jesus
in his glory, but he experienced great difficulty in staying with him
in his pain. Yet Peter, and the others as well, would come to learn,

not without much suffering themselves, that it is the mark of true friendship to be just as willing to share in the sorrows of a friend as it is to participate in the latter's moments of great joy.

"When a Friend Asks, There Is No Tomorrow"

Friendship means a willingness to be of assistance to one's friends. But friendships exist at different levels. And the quality of the friendship determines the degree to which a friend will go out of his or her way to help a friend in need. Jesus offers an example of a person who goes to a friend at midnight and asks for some food for a guest who has arrived unexpectedly (Lk 11:5–10). Jesus remarks that the friend in this case does not get out of bed because he is a friend, but because he grows weary of the persistence and importunity of the friend. The response of the friend in Jesus' example is quite different from that of the type of friend about whom the poet George Herbert somewhere writes: "When a friend asks, there is no tomorrow." Clearly, the deeper the friendship, the greater the willingness to make sacrifices in the name of friendship.

The most faithful and dearest of friends willingly bears any burden and makes any sacrifice out of love for a friend in need. Jesus expressed this truth about deep friendship in its starkest form when he said: "There is no greater love than this: to lay down one's life for one's friends" (Jn 15:13 NAB). John says of Jesus: "He had loved his own in this world, and would show his love for them to the end" (Jn 13:1 NAB). Just a few hours after Jesus told his disciples about the greatest love a friend could have for a friend, he put his teaching in practice by submitting to a most cruel death out of love for his friends and, indeed, for his enemies as well. It took Jesus' apostle-friends some time to learn to love in the radical way Jesus loved, but in the end, after receiving the gift of Jesus' Holy Spirit of love, they too loved in the same self-sacrificing manner as Jesus had loved them.

Permanence and Fidelity

Friendship at its deeper levels aspires to permanence and unswerving fidelity. Jesus reveals himself as the friend who remains faithful and true to his friends right to the end. "He remains faithful—for he cannot deny himself" (2 Tim 2:13). Among his disciple-friends Mary Magdalene mirrors the undeviating fidelity of her teacher-friend. In the fourth gospel Mary Magdalene is one of the few friends of Jesus who stand by him in his suffering and is not afraid to be known as a follower of this "accursed" one. And fidelity reaps the fruits that fidelity alone can bear. In her deep love Mary went early in the morning, while it was still dark, to the tomb of Jesus. John tells us that when Mary saw that the stone had been removed from the tomb she "ran" to let Peter and the beloved disciple know what had happened. A bit later Mary returns to the tomb and the risen Jesus reveals himself to her by calling her by name: "Jesus said to her, 'Mary.' She turned and said to him in Hebrew, 'Rab-boni!' (which means Teacher)" (Jn 20:16). Throughout history saints and scholars have constantly uncovered new layers of meaning in John's account of the revelatory encounter of Mary Magdalene and the risen Jesus in the garden. Yet, at its simplest level, what we recognize here is a friend, blessing a friend, for her unswerving fidelity and devotion at a time of greatest need.

The "Double Law" of Friendship

If friendship aspires to fidelity, friendship also naturally inclines a faithful friend to forgive a lapse in fidelity on the part of his or her friend. On the reverse side, when a close friend fails a friend in great need, the former can experience a repentant, sorrowing love of such intensity and sincerity that a mending of the rupture becomes possible and desirable for both the offended and offending friend. In the instance of the friendship between Jesus and Peter and the latter's infidelity, we see this "double law" of friendship most powerfully at work. Peter in his triple denial of Jesus caused his Lord and Wisdom-friend the most grievous suffering. Two brief verses in the gospel of Luke tellingly reveal the agony of the two friends at the moment of Peter's third denial of Jesus: "And the Lord turned and looked at Peter. And Peter remembered the word of the Lord, how he had said to him, 'Before the cock crows today, you will deny me three times.' And he went out and wept bitterly" (Lk 22:61–62). Jesus understood Peter's great sorrow over his infidelity. And, after the resurrection, John portrays Jesus as calling forth from Peter a triple affirmation of love: "He said to him the third time, 'Simon, son of John, do you love me?' Peter was grieved because he said to him the third time, 'Do you love me?' And he said to him, 'Lord, you know everything; you know that I love you' " (Jn 21:17). Jesus, through the "serious playfulness" of his questioning of Peter, transformed the sad event of the latter's triple denial into a happy opportunity for Peter's triple affirmation of love that forged forever the deepest bonds of friendship between them.

Jesus and Judas

Reflection on the healing of the rupture in friendship between Peter and Jesus can lead us to ponder the outcome of the break in friendship between Jesus and Judas. The betrayal of Jesus by Judas stands in stark contrast with the denials of Jesus by Peter because in the end scripture tells us nothing of reconciliation. It is not that Jesus gave up on Judas; rather, Judas seems to have given up on Jesus. Matthew's and Luke's accounts of Jesus' last words to Judas intimate that Jesus tried to the end to touch Judas' heart. In Luke, at the moment of betrayal, Jesus calls Judas by name, just as the latter moves to kiss him, and says: "Judas, would you betray the Son of man with a kiss?" (22:48). In Matthew, in the instant after Judas kisses him, Jesus says: "Friend, why are you here?" (26:50). Jesus, throughout his ministry, constantly used questioning as a means of challenging friend and foe alike to conversion or deeper transformation of mind and heart. In his piercing, immensely poignant questioning of Judas at the moment of his betrayal, Jesus makes a final effort to bring Judas to a repentant, sorrowing love. But, unlike Peter, Judas appears to give up hope in Jesus and in himself and in the end hangs himself.

William Sadler remarks that "Dante considered the love of friendship to be a sacred gift, one of the greatest treasures in life." He adds that

> in the final canto of the *The Inferno* there is a lugubrious description of the most horrible punishment inflicted upon any of the damned. Three individuals are eternally torn into shreds by the sharp teeth of Satan. The unpardonable sin for which they are tortured is no less than the betrayal of the bond of friendship. The three are Cassius, Brutus, and Judas Iscariot.[9]

Finally, of course, we can in hope entrust Judas to the unsearchable mercy of God, since "with God all things are possible" (Mt 19:26). But the histories of the friendships of Mary Magdalene, Peter, and Judas with Jesus remain as powerful symbols of the beauty of friendship in its full blossoming and of the great sadness of friendship lastingly betrayed.

Clearly, Jesus in his public ministry did not seek to *impose* wisdom and virtue on those who would be his friends. Yet, as *the* Wisdom-friend, he did gift them with an unsurpassed example of wise living, of loving wisely and an invitation to follow in his path, aided by his Spirit. Rollo May offers a description of four types of "love" ideally present in friendship and all other human love encounters. May's account aids us in contemplating Jesus as he integrated the basic forms of loving in his own daily living and sought to guide his friends to the love of wisdom and an ordered, wise loving.

Sexuality, Eros, Friendship, Agape

Psychologist Rollo May distinguishes between *sex, eros, philia* or *friendship,* and *agape.*[10] Sex refers basically to the gender of the person and physiological sexuality in its diverse expressions. Eros goes beyond the strictly sexual to include the "pull" of one person toward another; eros involves attraction and is the source of affection, tenderness, intimacy. Philia or friendship is "resting" and delight in the being of another person; it asks nothing of the other person except that he or she be himself or herself. Agape, for May, is a selfless, disinterested love and concern for the welfare of the other person. Interestingly, Bernard Lonergan, like May, also distinguishes between strictly physiological sexuality, eros, friendship and agape.[11] Lonergan, however, emphasizes the fact that agape is an unmerited divine grace, the supernatural gift of charity, through which a person becomes a friend of God and capable of loving friend and enemy alike, with a self-transcending love. Both May and Lonergan view sexuality, eros and friendship as authentic dimensions of human persons in their existing and interacting with others, but they both see the need for the integration of the lower by the higher, e.g. of eros by friendship and of the latter by agape.

Jesus: Chaste and Integrated in His Sexuality

The New Testament depicts Jesus as an individual healthy and whole in his sexuality. Jesus moves with ease in the company of male and female friends alike. He speaks freely about sexual issues and shows no squeamishness in dealing with prostitutes, adulterous individuals (Jn 8:3) or persons whom his society views as "unclean" (Mk 5:25). He does take strong positions about the need for fidelity in marriage and the avoidance of promiscuous activities (Mt 5:28). At the same time, for example, Jesus shows no discomfort about touching or being touched. He does not fear but rather invites intimacy. Jesus allows Mary to cover his feet with kisses and the beloved disciple to recline close to him at dinner (Jn 13:23). Overall, the New Testament, although not explicitly concerned with the issue of sexual integration, provides us with a portrait of Jesus as a man who was chaste, comfortable and integrated in his own sexuality.

May warns of the dangers of a sexuality not channeled and disciplined by eros; he likewise sees the need of the higher ordering of eros by friendship and agape.[12] Lonergan acknowledges the integrating role of friendship and agape in regard to sexuality and eros; but he also sees eros as "startled by a beauty" that shifts attention away from the self toward another.[13] "*Eros* leads to company" and "company reveals deeper qualities of mind and character to set up a human friendship."[14] The latter, in turn, disposes the heart for the higher gift of agape. Lonergan writes: "We have a dispositive upward tendency from *eros* to friendship, and from friendship to a special order of charity."[15] Lonergan, following Aquinas, describes "charity" or agape as "friendship in Christ."[16]

"Jesus Looked Steadily at Him and Loved Him"

The gospels, as we have seen, also present Jesus as a man capable of deep affection in his encounters with his friends and others. Doubtless, Jesus, like all other human beings, felt an instinctive attraction toward certain persons upon meeting them. For he was like us in every respect, but without sin (Heb 4:15). Friendships begin with a mutual attraction of some kind. In the case of Jesus' encounter with the rich man, who asked him what he should do to inherit eternal life, Mark recounts that "Jesus looked steadily at him and loved him" (Mk 10:21 Jerusalem Bible). Some scholars suggest that Jesus felt a special love for the rich man. He was spontaneously attracted to certain qualities he discerned in the rich man and invited him to follow him. But in Jesus eros and philia always existed in harmony with agape, and he saw the need to require of the rich man that he renounce his possessions if he was to become his disciple and friend. The rich man went away sad because, though he felt the spiritual magnetism of the Wisdom-teacher from Nazareth, he was not able to meet the requirements of total self-giving which Jesus set down as a condition for disciple-ship. No doubt Jesus was saddened too, but he would not and could not compromise the demands of agape for the sake of any lesser love, however attractive, excellent, worthwhile it might be.

Agape: The Ruling Love in Jesus' Friendships

Earlier we saw how deeply Jesus lived the reality of philia, of friendship during his public life. He formed deep affective bonds with Mary Magdalene, Martha, Lazarus, Peter, James, John and others. But agape was always the "ruling love" in Jesus' life and in his friendships. In speaking to his apostle-friends at the "supper of love" he told them clearly: "You are my friends if you do what I command you" (Jn 15:14). And what was the command of Jesus? It was to love with the love of agape: "This is my commandment, that you love one another as I have loved you" (Jn 15:12). In Jesus sexuality, eros, philia and agape existed in a fully integrated and harmonious unity. And whoever entered into a bond of friendship with Jesus was necessarily exposed to the powerful attraction of his example and the inner summons of his Holy Spirit to imitate him by striving to love in the same wise, integrated way that Jesus himself lived and loved.

Jesus: Unique Friend

Friendships, rooted in wisdom and expressed in orderly loving, respect the uniqueness and particular requirements of each indi-vidual friendship. Nowhere do we find this feature of friendship etched more sharply than in the instance of friendship with Jesus Christ. The true friend of Jesus recognizes the peerless quality of his friendship and experiences a profound reverence toward him. If it is true, as Thomas Aquinas remarks, that friendship requires a certain likeness between friends,[17] it is equally the case that friendship can exist only between those who are distinct from one another and acknowledge this distinctiveness. Simone Weil rightly says of any human friendship: "The two friends have fully con-sented to be two and not one, they respect the distance which the fact of being two distinct creatures places between them."[18] If this is true of any merely human friendship, it is uniquely apposite in the case of friendship with Jesus. In fact, in the same "last dis-course" in which Jesus called his apostles his friends, because he shared with them the deepest secrets of his heart, he also said to them: "You call me Teacher and Lord; and you are right, for so I am" (Jn 13:13). Jesus pointed out both the similarities and differences that existed between him and his apostle-friends.

Doubtless, the unprecedented nature of friendship with Jesus explains theologian Hans Urs von Balthasar's observation that "Paul never describes himself as a friend of Christ (although Jesus calls his disciples friends), but always as *doulos,* as his slave. 'You may call me friend,' says Augustine, 'I confess to be a servant.' "[19] Ignatius of Loyola, too, in his *Spiritual Exercises* echoes this instinctive Christian sense of the unparalleled quality of friendship with Jesus when he recommends that the retreatant engage in a prayerful conversation with Jesus, "by speaking exactly as one friend speaks to another, or as a servant speaks to a master."[20]

Yet, Jesus himself calls each of us by name (Jn 10:3) and addresses us as his "friends." It is for this reason that we "make bold" to call him "friend" in turn and to express both in our private prayers (Mt 6:6) and as a community our love for him as friend. The church too confirms us in our daring to call Jesus friend and to relate to him with the affections of a friend. In the liturgical celebration of the Holy Name the people of God pray: "May we who honor the holy name of Jesus enjoy his friendship in this life and be filled with eternal joy in his kingdom."

In the final analysis, then, the most gracious response we can make to Jesus, who calls us his friends, is to take him at his word and call him friend in return. Biblical scholar Xavier Leon-Dufour eloquently reminds us that Jesus has given "a face of flesh"[21] to God's loving friendship toward us. It is now our turn to let the love of Christ the friend manifest itself in our own lives by showing a generous, self-sacrificing love toward all others whom Jesus invites to share in his friendship.

Notes

1. Aelred of Rievaulx, *Spiritual Friendship,* translated by Mary Laker (Washington, D.C.: Cistercian Publications-Consortium Press, 1974), p. 65.

2. Bernard Lonergan, "The Dehellenization of Dogma," *A Second Collection* (London: Darton, Longman & Todd, 1974), p. 25.

3. Jaroslav Pelikan, *Jesus Through The Centuries* (New Haven: Yale University Press, 1985), p. 11.

4. Ibid.; cf. pp. 14–18.

5. Elisabeth Schüssler Fiorenza, *In Memory of Her* (New York: Crossroad Publishing Company, 1984), p. 135.

6. Ibid.; cf. pp. 132–134.

7. C. F. D. Moule, *The Origin of Christology* (Cambridge: Cambridge University Press, 1977), p. 176.

8. Cited by Ann Margaret Sharp, "Simone Weil on Friendship," *Philosophy Today* 22, Winter 1978, p. 270.

9. William A. Sadler, Jr., "The Experience of Friendship," *Humanitas* VI, No. 2, Fall 1970, p. 193.

10. Cf. Stephen Sundborg, *Sexual-Affective Integration in Celibacy: A Psycho-Spiritual Study of the Experience of Ruth Burrows in the Light of the Psychology of Rollo May*, a thesis completed at the Gregorian University, printed in an excerpted form (Rome: Gregorian University, 1984), pp. 10–14.

11. Bernard Lonergan, "Finality, Love, Marriage," *Collection* (New York: Herder and Herder, 1967), esp. pp. 30–31, 36–37, 45.

12. Cf. Stephen Sundborg, *Sexual Affective Integration in Celibacy*, p. 13.

13. Bernard Lonergan, "Finality, Love, Marriage," p. 31.

14. Ibid., p. 36.

15. Ibid., p. 31.

16. Ibid., p. 37.

17. Cf. Joseph Bobik, "Aquinas on Friendship with God," *New Scholasticism* 60, 1986, pp. 257–259.

18. Cited by Ann Margaret Sharp, "Simone Weil on Friendship," p. 269.

19. Hans Urs von Balthasar, *Does Jesus Know Us? Do We Know Him?* (San Francisco: Ignatius Press, 1983), p. 88.

20. Louis J., Puhl, S. J., *The Spiritual Exercises of St. Ignatius* (Chicago: Loyola University Press, 1951), p. 28.

21. Xavier Leon-Dufour, "Friend," *Dictionary of Biblical Theology* (New York: Seabury Press, 1973), p. 191.

6

Beloved and Lover

A striking blend of passion and tenderness tends to characterize martyrs and mystics alike in their expressions of love for Jesus Christ. Many saints easily interchange the images of Jesus as friend and as beloved or spouse when they seek to describe him as they image him in prayer. What justifies the martyrs, the mystics in their passionate and tender expressions of love for Jesus? What explains the imaging of those saints—female and male—who are as much at ease with the image of Jesus as spouse as they are with that of him as friend? Is this use of spousal imagery compatible with healthy sexuality or does it imply a repressed or distorted sexuality? Saint Augustine somewhere wrote: "Give me a lover and he [she] will catch my meaning." We can do no better than to focus on the experience and testimony of the saints to learn for ourselves that "logic of the heart," which, I believe, justifies the love-language and ways of imaging Jesus of martyrs, mystics, holy people.

The Passion of Ignatius of Antioch

One of the most striking examples of a martyr's passionate love for Jesus Christ is that of Saint Ignatius of Antioch. Ignatius was born about the time Jesus died, and he suffered martyrdom himself around A.D. 107. I read and reread as a young man the seven letters Ignatius wrote, as he was journeying in chains from Antioch to Rome, where he underwent martyrdom. Apart from holy scripture itself few Christian writings possess the beauty and power of the brief epistles of Ignatius of Antioch.

Ignatius writes with the same passionate intensity Paul shows in his epistles. Like Paul, Ignatius reveals a deep love of Jesus Christ. Though he is writing only seventy years after the death and resurrection of Jesus, Ignatius often speaks of "our God Jesus Christ."[1]

At the same time Ignatius stresses again and again the true humanity of Jesus Christ. He writes to the Magnesians: "I want you to be unshakably convinced of the Birth, the Passion, and the Resurrection which were the true and indisputable experiences of Jesus Christ, our Hope, in the days of Pontius Pilate's governorship."[2] Ignatius asks of the Ephesians: "Remember me, as Jesus Christ remembers you."[3] Ignatius' letters radiate friendly affection toward the communities to which he writes and toward individuals, such as Polycarp, the young bishop of the Smyrnaean church, who was eventually to follow in Ignatius' footsteps as a martyr. And although Ignatius does not explicitly call Jesus "friend," he shows the strong affection of a friend for a friend in his longing to be with Christ. He writes to the Romans: "I am yearning for death with all the passion of a lover."[4] He exclaims:

All the ends of the earth, all the kingdoms of the world would be of no profit to me; so far as I am concerned, to die in Jesus Christ is better than to be monarch of earth's widest bounds. He who died for us is all that I seek; He who rose again for us is my whole desire.[5]

There exists no more powerful expression of love for Jesus Christ and of communion in friendship with those who love Jesus than that of Ignatius of Antioch. Yet a great multitude of martyrs, animated with an equally passionate love for Jesus Christ, both preceded Ignatius and followed in his footsteps. Saint Blandina, for example, one of the martyrs of Lyons, encouraged those tortured before her and then was herself subjected to torture, but overcame because "of all she believed in and because of her intimacy with Christ."[6] The accounts of the early Christian martyrs—males and females alike—give testimony to the intense, intimate love of the martyrs for Jesus Christ and of their sense of equality and of friendship with one another in Christ.

Love of Jesus and *The Imitation of Christ*

In the ages following the time of Roman persecutions there was a flowering of friendships of holy people with Jesus and a manifestation of varied, rich dimensions of their love for him in their lives, deeds and writings. To make a "leap" across many centuries, nowhere perhaps does the gentle, endearing expression of an intimate love of Jesus Christ reveal itself more strikingly than in

Thomas a Kempis' fifteenth century work, *The Imitation of Christ*, one of the most widely read spiritual books, apart from the Bible itself.

The Imitation has two sections entitled, respectively, "Loving Jesus Above All Else," and "Close Friends With Jesus." Thomas a Kempis writes: "Love Jesus and keep Him as your Friend. . . . Hold fast to Jesus both in life and in death and commit yourself to His steadfast love, for He alone can help you when all others fail. Your Beloved is such that He admits no rival."[7] The author writes further: "To be without Jesus is a painful hell but to be with Him is a sweet paradise. . . . Whoever finds Jesus discovers a wonderful treasure, a treasure above all others, and [the one] who loses Jesus loses a great deal—more than the entire world."[8] And the author advises: "It is a great art to know how to live with Jesus, and to know how to keep His friendship demands great wisdom. Be humble and peace-loving and Jesus will be with you. Be devout and calm and Jesus will abide with you." He adds: "Of all those whom you hold dear, let Jesus alone be your most special friend."[9]

A Hymn to Love

The Imitation describes the qualities of the love of Jesus in words matched in their beauty perhaps only by Paul's hymn to charity in the thirteenth chapter of his first epistle to the Corinthians:

> Love wishes to soar to the heights. . . . There is nothing sweeter than love, nothing stronger, nothing more sublime, more robust, nor better in heaven or on earth. . . . [The one] in love flies high, runs swiftly, and overflows with joy. . . . Love knows no measure but exceeds all measure. . . . Love keeps watch, and even while resting it sleeps not. . . . Like a living flame and burning torch, love always makes its way upward into the open air and blazes forth. . . . Whoever is in love recognizes love's voice. . . . Love is swift, honest, devout, pleasing. . . . It is strong, patient, faithful, prudent. . . . Love is cautious, humble and upright. . . . It is sober, chaste, steadfast, tranquil.[10]

I should add that the love *The Imitation* describes is a generative love, a love that "is noble and urges us to perform great deeds and excites us to always desire what is more perfect."[11] All authentic Christian love seeks to manifest itself in "deeds of love," though

the greatest deeds may be the prayers of the holy ones that are
most powerful before God (Jas 5:16) and move mountains.

The Imitation likewise portrays the love of Jesus, as friend, as an
absolutely unique love, a love that admits no rivals. What Saint
Francis de Sales says of our love of God applies equally to our love
of Jesus, who is our Lord and God (Jn 20:28). Francis states that
we love God with a special love. Our love for God and Jesus "is a
love of friendship, a friendship of affection, an affection of preference, but a preference that is unrivaled, supreme."[12]

Prayer: "Love-Making" Between the Soul and God

Another feature of the friendship of holy people and especially
mystics with Christ is the use of nuptial language to describe the
relationship between the believer and Jesus. Catherine de Hueck
Doherty, for example, characterizes prayer as "love-making" between the soul and God.[13] This kind of language roots itself in holy
scripture itself. The Song of Songs, for example, although it was
perhaps originally a poem celebrating the love of man and woman,
became a source-text for mystics seeking symbols to depict the
love between God and humankind, between Christ and the believer. Interestingly, the Song of Songs is accepted by Jewish,
Protestant and Catholic believers alike as an integral part of holy
scripture. Indeed, historian Jaroslav Pelikan cites the Rabbi
Aquiba, who stated at the council of Jamnia in 90 C.E.: "The
whole world is not worth the day on which the Song of Songs was
given to Israel, for all the Scriptures are holy, but the Song of
Songs is the Holy of Holies."[14]

It is important to recognize that the Song of Songs was not just
valued from early times by celibates, but that it probably finds its
authorship among lay persons who valued the beauty of human
love as a gift of God. It is equally significant that married Jews
were among the first to see the love of male and female as an
emblem of the love of God and humankind. The primal image of
God as lover comes, then, most likely not from celibates but from
married individuals.

Moreover, the contemporary scholarly married couple, Drs.
Ann and Barry Ulanov, reveal in their own beautiful writings on
prayer and psychology a profound appreciation of the power of
marital imagery to express the spiritual. They write:

The spiritual dimension of sexuality, built upon and never excluding the bodily and emotional parts, expands sexuality to emphasize the mark of otherness in this intimate touching of selves. Perhaps that is one reason why sexual metaphors reflecting the world of the flesh turn up so often as the major language of the great mystics to describe their most rapturous meetings with God.

They further remark that "in sexuality, as in all else, we allow our utter dependency on God to come to the fore. . . . The images of God as spouse and lover come easily as we seek to be taken into God's love and to open to it."[15]

Holy scripture does not hesitate to speak of God as "lover of souls" (Wis 11:26 NAB), of human beings as "lovers of God" (2 Tim 3:4), of Jesus as "beloved" (Mt 12:18), of God (Is 62:5) and Jesus (Mt 9:15) as bridegroom and of the church as "bride" (Rev 21:9). It is not surprising that as Christians came to recognize the divinity of Christ they found it easy to apply the Hebrew Testament image of God as spousal lover to Jesus himself. I thus feel justified in freely citing the saints in their use of the language of lover and beloved, of nuptial images charged with tenderness, beauty and passion, as it seems appropriate.

Spousal Mysticism and the Equality of Women

Yet, since the use of nuptial language in reference to God and Christ causes problems for some today, I would like to preface my citation of saints and poets who use nuptial symbols with some remarks about the appropriateness of such language.

Some object that the description of God and Christ as bridegroom and the church and individuals as bride suggests an inferior status of women in relationship to men. Yet in 1948 Dorothy Day wrote:

The love of God and man becomes the love of equals as the love of the bride and the bridegroom is the love of equals, and not the love of the sheep for the shepherd, or the servant for the master, or the child for the parent. We may stand at times in the relationship of servant, and at other times in that of child, as far as our feelings go and in our present state. But the

relationship we hope to attain is that of the love of the Canticle of Canticles.[16]

More recently, Diane Tennis in her book *Is God the Only Reliable Father?* recounts that, as she struggled with the text in the
Ephesian letter where wives are told to regard their husbands *"as
they regard the Lord,"* she reflected that Jesus, the Lord, was a
man who did not cling to power, but gave it up and became a
servant (Phil 2:6–7). Thus, "the model 'Lord' of the household of
faith is neither a taskmaster nor a benevolent despot. The model
Lord of the household is a servant."[17] In this context, then, one
might ask: "Is Jesus the only reliable bridegroom?" I suggest that
the metaphor of Jesus as bridegroom is salvageable and even of
value in prayer, if Jesus as bridegroom is understood against the
background of his total acceptance of women as equals to men in
the kingdom and of his role as one who serves.

Psycho-Sexual Problems and Imaging Christ as Spouse

Others caution that psycho-sexual problems can arise for some
in their imaging of God and Christ as spouse. Sandra Schneiders
remarks that, from a Freudian perspective, in males who relate to
Christ as spouse a sublimated renunciation of their own sexual
identity may be required. At the same time, Schneiders observes
that "much of the most beautiful mystical literature celebrating
the marriage of the soul with Jesus has come from the pens of male
mystics who experienced themselves as the bride" and she acknowledges that "there is something quite valid in the realization
that total receptivity is the basis of mutuality in love." But she adds
that "the problem has been in defining such receptivity as exclusively feminine and divine self-gift as exclusively masculine."[18]
Schneiders concludes on a very positive note in remarking that not
only have women mystics "experienced the height and depth and
length and breadth of loving mutuality with the divine spouse,"
but "they have also experienced the mysterious femininity of
Jesus who gives birth to his Church from his own side and feeds
his disciples from his own body, thus mystically revealing the special God-likeness that women enjoy through their capacity to
give life."[19]

Contemplative Prayer and Imaging Jesus as Spouse

The psychologist Ignace Lepp in his classic *The Psychology of
Loving* observes that "while certain false mystics . . . manifest

unmistakable evidence of experiencing a sexual orgasm during their 'ecstasy,' there is never the slightest indication that this is so in the case of Saint John of the Cross, Saint Teresa of Avila, or any other genuine mystic."[20] Psychologist Gerald May, however, remarks that "in contemplative prayer for example, it is not unusual for men to experience erections and for women also to experience genital stimulation—sometimes even to the point of orgasm."[21]

Gerald May warns about the limitations of all images of God and the need on the part of both sexes to deal in a healthy way with erotic, genital experiences that can occur in prayer. May suggests that it is more often the case that sexual feelings that occur in prayer are ways of expressing longing for union with the divine, rather than simply substitutes for actual sexual experience with another human being.[22]

May also remarks that from a Jungian perspective Christian contemplatives "consistently viewed the human soul as the feminine principle—the bride—and the divine (God, Jesus, or Holy Spirit) as the masculine principle, the bridegroom." He adds that "from their writings, it appears that men handled this imagery quite as well as women, having no difficulty in seeing their souls as deeply in love with, embraced by, and in union with a masculine God." May himself sees the "final contemplative option" as a "going beyond the images altogether, into that beyond-place where maleness and femaleness are not dualized but are simple expedient facets of the ultimate One."[23]

An Integrally Chaste Way of Praying

Now, in instances where individuals do experience sexual arousal in prayer, I think that the contemplators neither should panic nor should they actively encourage these phenomena. On the other hand, they should not deny the reality of these experiences or flee from them in a way that encourages repression. Rather, they should seek with the help of a spiritual director or counselor to understand what is happening and to deal with what they experience in a creative, healthy way. Little by little, with God's aid, they should seek to move toward that degree of integration in which the highest levels of the spirit exercise a sweet dominion over the psychological and somatic dimensions of the person. For, clearly, if chastity is an authentic Christian value, then those who pray should seek especially to foster an integrally chaste way of praying. They should strive with God's help to learn how to let go *gently* of those forms of fantasizing, imaging which do not promote ever higher levels of self-forgetfulness, of self-transcendence in communing with God. Their goal should be that which John of the Cross describes in the last stanza of his poem *The Dark Night:*

I abandoned and forgot myself,
Laying my face on my Beloved;
All things ceased; I went out from myself,
Leaving my cares
Forgotten among the lilies.[24]

Persons, however, such as those I have just described, should seek to avoid endless neurotic self-recriminations because they do not yet experience complete personal integration. They should also resist the temptation to give up praying altogether, though with a spiritual director's or counselor's advice they may need to avoid certain forms of praying for a time. Most importantly, they should not allow themselves to develop a contempt for the body or sexual desire. They should recognize that the gift of complete spiritual, psychological and somatic integration is for most human beings a goal toward which they aspire rather than an actual achievement. Rather, in the spirit of the famous *Serenity Prayer,* they should ask God to grant them the serenity to accept humbly those undesirable aspects of themselves that they cannot yet change, the courage to change those perturbing dimensions of themselves they can presently change, and the wisdom to know the difference.

In terms of my own experience and study, I find that men or women who relate to Jesus as lover or spouse do not inevitably interpret the metaphor in a rather literal fashion and hence do not necessarily experience sexual problems or anxiety in this prayer-context. Rather, Jesus, who is both God and man, stands revealed to many, under the metaphor of spouse or lover, as one who loves deeply, tenderly, totally, ecstatically, without any reservations. My own advice is: Let the one who finds delight in the symbol of Jesus as spouse or lover embrace *him* through this image. If the love that blossoms from this embrace is chaste, integrative, generative and self-sacrificing, then it is surely a gift from God; hence one need have no anxiety, but only thankfulness, as she or he abides prayerfully in the presence of Jesus, spouse and lover.

The More Perfect Image of Jesus: Friend or Spouse?

Some theologians ask: What is the most perfect image of the loving union of the human being with Christ, with God? Is it the image of friendship or the image of marriage? Martin Darcy in his modern classic *The Mind and Heart of Love* argues that "the perfection of love . . . is to be found in personal friendship." Darcy proposes that this is the case, whether the friendship involved is that between a man and a woman, between two individuals of the same sex or between human beings and God.[25] Blessed Edith Stein, however, suggests that "the eternal purpose for which God has created the soul is a relationship with him that could not be described more accurately than by a bridal union."[26]

Significantly, among the images that the saints and particularly the mystics most often link together in naming Jesus are those of friend and spouse, friend and beloved, friend and lover. I believe this happens because in spousal friendship, in friendship between lover and beloved, the basic characteristics of friendship find their most exquisite, intense, glorious expression. Thus, John of the Cross, toward the end of his commentary on *The Spiritual Canticle*, where he is describing the most sublime union of the soul with God, writes:

> The property of love is to make the lover equal to the object loved. Since the soul in this state possesses perfect love, she is called the bride of the Son of God, which signifies equality with Him. In this equality of friendship the possessions of both are held in common, as the Bridegroom Himself said to His disciples: "I have now called you my friends, because all that I have heard from my Father I have manifested to you" (Jn 15:15).[27]

We need not then see a contradiction between the views of Martin Darcy and Edith Stein. Rather, we can simply envisage marriage as expressing the characteristics of human friendship in their most intense, ecstatic form.

The delighting love of Jesus, as beloved and friend, that *The Imitation* depicts so beautifully is a love that seeks and desires union, indeed, unique union with Jesus. St. Francis de Sales teaches that in friendship attraction awakens love, love seeks union, and the highest union is that of charity. Saint Catherine of

Siena finds it appropriate to use the language of lover and beloved
to describe the completeness of union that friends seek with Jesus.
In *The Dialogue* Catherine puts these words on the lips of the
Father, as he speaks to her about Jesus, whom he calls "my
Truth": "My Truth said in these words: 'He who loves me shall be
one thing with me and I with him.' " The Father continues: "This
is the state of two dear friends, for though they are two in body,
yet they are one in soul through the affection of love, because love
transforms the lover into the object loved."[28] Saint John of the
Cross in his poem *The Dark Night* expresses the language of loving
union with Christ in yet more exquisite symbols:

> O guiding night!
> O night more lovely than the dawn!
> O night that has united
> The Lover with His beloved,
> Transforming the beloved in her Lover.[29]

The Imitation too focuses on the unique I-Thou relationship between Jesus and the believer and it uses interchangeably the titles
"friend," "lover," "beloved" in naming Jesus and the one who
loves him.

A Unique Love

The saints, in describing their relationship with their beloved,
tell us that, just as they love Jesus with a preference that is "unrivaled, supreme," so they also experience themselves as loved by
Jesus in their uniqueness. Jesus deepens the individual's sense of
his or her own unique identity in the special love he shows to each
holy one in prayer. In John, Jesus says that if any person loves him,
he, in turn, will reveal himself to that person (Jn 14:21). Bernard
of Clairvaux was acutely aware of the particularity of the relationship between Jesus and himself. He wrote: "And each finds a
secret for herself with the Bridegroom, and says: My secret is
mine, my secret is mine."[30]

Jesus' love of each person in his or her uniqueness does not
militate against his love for others in their uniqueness nor is it the
cause of jealousy or envy among the holy ones. In the words of
Elizabeth Barrett Browning's *Sonnet XXI From the Portuguese:*
"Who can fear too many stars, though each in heaven shall roll—
Too many flowers, though each shall crown the year?"[31] Doubt-

less, the friend of Jesus does at times ask him in prayer, as Elizabeth requests of her human beloved: "Say thou dost love me, love me, love me—toll the silver interance!"[32] But the true friend of Jesus loves and is loved with a love that embraces all in their uniqueness. As Augustine says to the Lord: "Blessed whoso loveth Thee, and his friend in Thee. . . . For he alone loses none dear to him, to whom all are dear in Him who cannot be lost."[33]

The love of Jesus and of those who love Jesus and all others in him is individual, but not individualistic. As Gilbert Meilaender observes: "If I read Augustine correctly, what we can learn from him is that real love for any human being, requiring as it does a disciplining of the selfish impulses, will begin to create in us a new openness toward others."[34] And this is, above all, the case in the mutual love between the believer and Jesus because Jesus makes it a condition of friendship with him that we love others, just as he loves them.

Each age has its own particular religious sensibility and perception of what is appropriate in the expression of feeling. Individuals too differ greatly in the ways they feel and articulate their feelings. *The Imitation* has had a profound effect on the formation of the spiritualities of such saints as Ignatius of Loyola and Francis de Sales, to name but two among many. But these latter saints each appropriated the sentiments of *The Imitation* in accord with their own temperaments and experiences. Each reader must do likewise, for what attracts one person in *The Imitation* or in other spiritual writings may leave another quite unmoved. Ignatius of Loyola, for example, unlike John of the Cross, Teresa of Avila and so many other great Christian mystics, did not choose to express his friendship with Jesus Christ in nuptial terms; yet his love for Jesus was just as ardent, passionate, all-consuming as that of John and Teresa.

A Sorrowing Love

Another feature that shines forth in the passionately tender friendships of Ignatius, Teresa, John of the Cross and other saints with Jesus is the special way they relate to him in his sufferings and death on the cross.

Ignatius invites the person engaged in making his *Spiritual Exercises* to contemplate, at a certain stage of the *Exercises*, "what Christ our Lord suffers,"[35] and prayerfully to ask "for sorrow with Christ in sorrow, anguish with Christ in anguish, tears and deep grief because of the great affliction Christ endures for me."[36] Ignatius suggests that the person making the retreat also consider "what I ought to do and suffer for Him."[37] Ignatius, like the early martyr bishop, Ignatius of Antioch, was gifted with a passionate love for Jesus in his suffering and a desire to take up the cross of his friend and follow him. Ignatius intends the *Spiritual Exercises*, in part, as a means of drawing others into the contemplation of the sufferings of Christ. He hopes that this contemplation will evoke a new way of feeling in the contemplator and, consequently, a new way of acting toward all who suffer.

John of the Cross wrote that "two things . . . serve the soul as wings to rise to union with God: sincere compassion with the death of Jesus and with its [the soul's] neighbor."[38] And in his sixteenth *Maxim on Love* John said simply: "Be a friend of the passion of Christ."[39] Blessed Edith Stein writes that John of the Cross not only felt profound compassion for Jesus in his sufferings, but that he had a very deep love for the "sick, the suffering members of Jesus Christ, throughout his life."[40] John's love for Jesus as a suffering friend was clearly a generative, fruitful love. Thus when, as a religious superior, John came into a monastery, "his first attention was given to the sick: he would prepare their food with his own hands, empty their slops" and not "allow them" to be taken away to a "hospital" in order to save money.[41]

Edith Stein observes that John of the Cross was an artist, a painter, as well as a poet. She remarks that "there is scarcely a believing artist who will never have felt the urge to represent Christ crucified or carrying his Cross." But she adds that "from the artist, too, the Crucified Lord demands more than such an image." He requires that the artist should "form himself, and let himself be formed, into the image of him who bore the Cross and died on it."[42] John of the Cross was such an artist.

Teresa of Avila, like Ignatius of Loyola and John of the Cross, experienced a special love of friendship for Jesus in his passion and she gave herself for others in a self-sacrificing love. She mentions that the example of Jesus in his passion supported her in her own sufferings. She writes: "When we are . . . suffering persecutions or trials . . . we have a very good Friend in Christ. . . . We think of His moments of weakness and times of trial; and He becomes our Companion."[43] In fact, "with so good a Friend . . . Who came forward first of all to suffer, one can bear everything. He helps us; He gives us strength; He never fails; He is a true Friend."[44] And the friends of Christ can in turn help others: "He needs His friends to be strong so that they may uphold the weak."[45] Authentic love of Jesus is a generative love that overflows into the support of others.

A Rejoicing Love

If the holy ones stand out in their love for Jesus as friend in his sufferings, they equally reveal in their lives a joy-filled love for Jesus as friend in his resurrection and exaltation in glory. In the final phase of his *Spiritual Exercises* Ignatius of Loyola recommends to those making the retreat that they contemplate Jesus in the mysteries of his resurrection and ask in prayer "for the grace to be glad and rejoice intensely because of the great joy and the glory of Christ."[46] Ignatius also suggests that they consider the risen Christ as "consoler" and compare the ways Jesus consoles "with the way in which friends are wont to console each other."[47] In this way the love of Jesus as consoling friend leads to the joyous consoling of all others as friends held fast in the love of Christ, the friend.

Christ consoles his friends in very special ways through the revelation of his goodness, his truth, his inner unity, his beauty. The theme of the glory of God and the beauty of Christ shines forth with a special clarity in the lives and writings of the mystics and holy poets. These latter, in turn, draw upon holy scripture as the ultimate source of inspiration for their joyous celebration of the glory and beauty of Christ—Wisdom-friend, Beloved, Spouse.

The author of the book of Wisdom writes that "there is immortality in kinship with Wisdom, and good pleasure in her friendship" (Wis 8:17 NAB); Solomon loved Wisdom as a youth and "was enamored of her beauty" (Wis 8:2). The gospels, as we have seen, portray Jesus as Wisdom-friend. The later scriptural writings speak of Christ as Wisdom itself (1 Cor 1:24). John speaks of the eternal Word, the Wisdom of God made flesh, as "full of grace and truth" (Jn 1:14) and radiating the glory of God. Hebrews likewise describes Jesus as the one who "reflects the glory of God and bears the very stamp of his nature" (Heb 1:3).

Francis, Clare and the Beauty of Christ

Francis and Clare of Assisi and John of the Cross enjoyed the gift of a most rare sensitivity to the beauty of the glorified Christ and of all creation. But, in each instance, a radical sharing in the "empty-

ing" of Christ (Phil 2:7) accompanied the gift of unique appreciation of the beauty of the risen Christ in his glory.

In becoming a "troubador" of Holy Poverty Francis experienced all creatures as his friends and as bearers of the imprint of
the beauty of his Beloved. He sings of Sister Moon and the stars
who are "precious and beautiful" and of Brother Fire who is
"beautiful and playful and robust and strong."[48] Francis tells those
who would follow Jesus in his poverty that they are "spouses,
brothers, and mothers of Our Lord Jesus Christ"[49] and that Jesus is
the "eternally victorious and glorified" one "upon Whom 'the
angels desire to gaze' (1 Pet 1:12)."[50]

Saint Bonaventure perhaps best describes the heart of Francis:
"In beautiful things he saw Beauty itself" and "he followed his
Beloved everywhere" by "making from all things a ladder by
which he could climb up and embrace him who is utterly desirable."[51] Yet, though Francis sang joyfully of the beauty of creation
and of Christ, he was no sentimentalist. He literally bore the
wounds of the crucified—the stigmata—in his flesh and led a life
harsh in its renunciations. He spent his last years blind and in great
suffering, but also full of hope and charity.

Perhaps no friendship among the saints has so gripped the
human imagination as that between Francis and Clare. Clare followed Francis in his radical imitation of the poverty of the Lord
and she too was blessed with an exquisite appreciation of the
beauty and glory of the risen Christ, her Beloved, along with an
intense sharing in his sufferings.

We have few writings of Clare, but "this poverty of sources . . .
is very much in keeping with the life of Clare, for it shows her total
absorptions in the mystery of Christ and her desire to imitate Him
in poverty and humility."[52] Clare writes to Agnes of Prague, a
sister of the king of Bohemia, who like Clare chose to live a life of
prayer and poverty:

> *Transform* your whole being *into the image* of the Godhead
> Itself through contemplation! So that you too may feel what
> His friends feel as they taste *the hidden sweetness* which God
> Himself has reserved from the beginning for those who love
> Him.[53]

Shortly before her death, Clare wrote to Agnes: "I rejoice and
exult with you in *the joy of the Spirit* (1 Thes 1:6), O Bride of
Christ." She continues: "Happy, indeed, is she to whom it is given

to share this sacred banquet" and "to cling with all her heart to Him Whose beauty all the heavenly hosts admire unceasingly. . . . Whose graciousness is our joy. . . . Whose remembrance brings a gentle light. . . . Whose fragrance will revive the dead" and "whose glorious vision will be the happiness of all the citizens of the heavenly Jerusalem."[54] But, despite the poetic sentiment and joy Clare here expresses, she, too, like Francis, experienced prolonged and severe sufferings during her life. Clare and Francis could both rightly apply to themselves the words of Paul: "For as we share abundantly in Christ's sufferings, so through Christ we share abundantly in comfort too (2 Cor 1:5).

The Mystical Love of John of the Cross

John of the Cross, like Francis and Clare of Assisi, was also gifted with a most remarkable sensitivity to beauty in all its manifestations, and, most especially, to the beauty of Christ, friend and beloved beyond all others. But John likewise followed the two saints of Assisi in seeking to free himself, with the help of God's grace, from all external and internal attachments to creatures. He is thus known not only as the greatest Spanish poet, but also as the mystic of the "dark night of the soul" and the teacher and practicer of the most radical forms of detachment from all created things.

The severity of John's teaching on self-denial reveals itself when he writes that a person "will be unable to reach perfection who does not strive to be content with having nothing."[55] John understands well the truth of Jesus' paradoxical teaching about the need to lose one's life in order to find it. John expresses this truth in his own inimitable way when he says:

To come to possess all
desire the possession of nothing.
To arrive at being all
desire to be nothing.[56]

In his *Spiritual Canticle* John reveals that he is well on his way in his quest to lose himself in order to find himself in the All that is the Beloved. He likewise manifests his incomparable poetic talent. Gerard Manley Hopkins, in one of his poems, speaks of God as "beauty's self and beauty's giver."[57] God's greatest gift of love was Jesus and the Holy Spirit and John makes the celebration of the beauty of the Eternal Word the highpoint of his *Spiritual Canticle* where he exclaims:

> Let us rejoice, Beloved,
> And let us go forth to behold ourselves in Your
> Beauty.[58]

John, in commenting on these verses, states:

> This means: . . . I shall see You in Your beauty, and You shall see me in Your beauty, and I shall see myself in You in Your beauty, and You will see Yourself in me in Your beauty. . . . Wherefore I shall be You in Your beauty, and You will be me in Your beauty, because your very beauty will be my beauty; and therefore we shall behold each other in Your beauty.[59]

Although John was blessed with the most exalted mystical graces and a sublime experience of his friend and beloved, Jesus, he, like Jesus, and Francis and Clare, suffered greatly in his last days. But he bore his suffering patiently, and forgave those who had persecuted and mistreated him.

The Powerful Prayer of the Saints

Finally, the passionate, tender love of John and other mystics for Jesus Christ is a highly generative love. There is a theme, woven through the Hebrew Testament and the New Testament, that strikingly portrays the great power for good in the world of righteous and prayerful individuals.

In Genesis, for example, we have the famous dialogue between Abraham and the Lord. God tells Abraham that he is going to destroy Sodom, but Abraham wins the promise from God that he will spare the city if there are fifty righteous people living there. Abraham then says: "Suppose five of the fifty righteous are lacking? Wilt thou destroy the whole city for lack of five?" Again, God relents and promises to spare the city. The "holy bartering" between God and Abraham continues until the Lord finally promises: "For the sake of ten I will not destroy it" (Gen 18:16–33). In the New Testament in the epistle of James we find the biblical author stressing that "the prayer of a righteous man has great power in its effects" (Jas 5:16). This brief sampling of biblical texts suggests that the existence of righteous people in the world makes a difference.

Clearly, the beneficial effects of the prayers of the righteous may not always be apparent to us. God's ways are not our ways (Rom 11:33) and God often responds to requests made in prayer in a fashion that seems to go against our deepest longings. But this does not mean that the prayers of the righteous go unanswered. Jesus, though he prayed to be delivered, if possible, from his enemies, was not spared the horror of death through crucifixion. But the Abba answered his beloved Son's prayer by raising him from the dead and crowning him with glory.

John of the Cross, toward the end of his *Spiritual Canticle*, writes:

> Now I occupy my soul
> And all my energy in His service;
> I no longer tend the herd,
> Nor have I any other work
> Now that my every act is love.[60]

John is here describing the holy person who has completely surrendered to Christ the Bridegroom, without keeping anything back. He indicates that when the soul, the "bride," reaches this point "a little of this pure love is more precious to God and the soul and more beneficial to the church, even though it seems one is doing nothing, than all these other [exterior apostolic works] put together.[61]

Certainly there exists a wide diversity of charisms among God's people. There is room for Dorothy Day in her Hospitality House, for Oscar Romero in his work for the poor, and for the anonymous contemplatives who spend their lives in the solitude of the cloister, praying for the healing and salvation of humanity. In the case of all of these individuals they can say with Paul: "The love of Christ impels us who have reached the conviction that since one died for all, all died. He died for all so that those who live might live no longer for themselves, but for him who for their sakes died and was raised up" (2 Cor 5:14–15).

Notes

1. Ignatius of Antioch, *Early Christian Writings*, translated by Maxwell Staniforth (Baltimore: Penguin Books, 1972), p. 103.

2. Ibid., p. 90.

3. Ibid., 82.

4. Ibid., p. 106.

5. Ibid., p. 105.

6. Herbert Musurillo, "The Martyrs of Lyons," *The Acts of the Christian Martyrs*, p. 81.

7. Thomas a Kempis, *The Imitation of Christ*, translated by Joseph Tylenda (Wilmington, Delaware: Michael Glazier, Inc., 1984), p. 89.

8. Ibid., p. 90.

9. Ibid., pp. 90–91.

10. Ibid., pp. 117–119.

11. Ibid., p. 117.

12. Francis de Sales, *The Love of God*, p. 109.

13. Catherine de Hueck Doherty, *Soul of My Soul* (Notre Dame: Ave Maria Press, 1985), p. 121.

14. Jaroslav Pelikan, *Jesus Through the Centuries* (New Haven: Yale University Press, 1985), p. 125.

15. Ann and Barry Ulanov, *Primary Speech: A Psychology of Prayer* (Atlanta: John Knox Press, 1982), p. 81.

16. Dorothy Day, *By Little and By Little*, edited by Robert Ellsberg (New York: Alfred A. Knopf, 1983), p. 227.

17. Diane Tennis, *Is God the Only Reliable Father?* (Philadelphia: The Westminster Press, 1985), p. 107.

18. Sandra M. Schneiders, *Women and the Word* (New York: Paulist Press, 1986), p. 66.

19. Ibid., p. 67.

20. Ignace Lepp, *The Psychology of Loving*, trans. by Bernard B. Gilligan (Baltimore: Helicon, 1963), p. 218.

21. Gerald May, *Will and Spirit* (San Francisco: Harper and Row, 1982), p. 150.

22. Ibid., pp. 150–151.

23. Ibid., p. 148.

24. John of the Cross, *The Collected Works of St. John of the Cross*, trans. by Kieran Kavanaugh and Otilio Rodriguez (Washington, D.C.: Institute of Carmelite Studies, 1973), p. 712.

25. Martin Darcy, *The Mind and Heart of Love* (London: Faber and Faber Limited, 1954), pp. 32–33.

26. Edith Stein, *The Science of the Cross*, translated by Hilda Graef (Chicago: Henry Regnery Company, 1960), p. 183.

27. John of the Cross, *The Collected Works of St. John of the Cross*, ibid., p. 520.

28. Catherine of Siena, *The Dialogue of the Seraphic Virgin Catherine of Siena* (New York: Benziger Brothers, 1925), p. 111.

29. John of the Cross, p. 711.

30. Cf. Jean Leclercq, *The Influence of Saint Bernard* (Oxford: S.L.G. Press, 1976), p. 5.

31. Elizabeth Barrett Browning *Poems of Elizabeth Barrett Browning: Vol. I* (New York: James Miller, 1869), p. 412.

32. Ibid.

33. Augustine, *The Confessions of St. Augustine*, (New York: Pocket Books Inc., 1957), p. 53.

34. Gilbert Meilaender, *Friendship: A Study in Theological Ethics* (Notre Dame: Notre Dame Press, 1981), p. 31.

35. Louis Puhl, *The Spiritual Exercises of St. Ignatius* (Chicago: Loyola University Press, 1951), p. 82.

36. Ibid., p. 84.

37. Ibid., p. 82.

38. Edith Stein, *The Science of the Cross*, p. 216.

39. John of the Cross, *The Collected Works of St. John of the Cross*, p. 675.

40. Edith Stein, *The Science of the Cross*, p. 217.

41. Ibid.

42. Ibid., pp. 3–4.

43. Teresa, *The Complete Works of Saint Teresa of Jesus: Vol. I*, p. 140.

44. Ibid., p. 139.

45. Ibid., p. 90.

46. Louis Puhl, *The Spiritual Exercises of St. Ignatius*, p. 95.

47. Ibid., p. 96.

48. Francis and Clare of Assisi, *Francis and Clare: The Complete Works*, translated by Regis J. Armstrong and Ignatius Brady (New York: Paulist Press, 1982), pp. 38–39.

49. Ibid., p. 63.

50. Ibid., p. 57.

51. Ibid., pp. 19–20.

52. Ibid., p. 174.

53. Ibid., p. 200.

54. Ibid., pp. 204–205.

55. John of the Cross, *The Collected Works of St. John of the Cross*, p. 671.

56. Ibid., p. 103.

57. Gerard Manley Hopkins, *Gerard Manley Hopkins*, selection of poems with introduction and notes by W. H. Gardner (Baltimore: Penguin Books, 1958), p. 54.

58. John of the Cross, *The Collected Works of St. John of the Cross*, p. 546.

59. Ibid., p. 547.

60. Ibid., p. 520.

61. Ibid., p. 523.

7

Abiding Presence in Friendships

Aelred of Rievaulx writes his treatise *Spiritual Friendship* in the form of a dialogue, and the first words he addresses to Ivo, his initial partner in conversation, are these: "Here we are, you and I, and I hope a third, Christ, is in our midst."[1] Aelred recognizes that Jesus is not only the friend whom we cherish most and the beloved in whose goodness and beauty we delight; Jesus is also a "third," a living, indwelling presence in all our friendships in the Lord. Indeed, Aelred is inspired by the "Spirit of Love" to tell Ivo that each friendship ought to "begin in Christ, continue in Christ, and be perfected in Christ."[2]

The Gift-Quality of Our Friendships

Jesus not only enters into friendship with us and dwells within our friendships. He also gifts us with the particular friendships we enjoy in his name. A theme that runs through the lives and writings of the saints is a sense of the gift-quality of the particular friendships in Christ we enjoy in this life. Biographers, for example, tell us that Saint Jane de Chantal saw Francis de Sales in a kind of "vision" before she actually met him, and that when she heard him preach she recognized him from the "vision."[3] Francis de Sales, in turn, after his first encounter with Jane, left her a note saying, "God, I am feeling, has given me to you. That is all I can say."[4] Again, Saint Margaret Mary Alacoque recounts in a letter that Jesus told her in an interior spiritual experience: "I will send you my faithful servant and perfect friend who will teach you to know Me."[5] During his first visit at the convent where Margaret Mary lived, she recognized Saint Claude de La Colombiere as the perfect friend whom Jesus had promised to send her. In their first meeting they spoke together for a lengthy period. Soon after, Claude said of her: "She is a soul of grace."[6]

130

The examples I have just offered of the gift-quality of friendships in Christ are taken from special experiences of saints. Doubtless, there exists skepticism today on the part of many about the "objectivity" of the types of spiritual experiences that Jane de Chantal, Margaret Mary Alacoque and others describe. But, however one might characterize such experiences, there is still very much alive today, among many believers, a profound sense of the gift-quality of the friendships they enjoy. Elsewhere, I have written about what I call the "sacrament of the present person"[7] and the providential character of every encounter we have with other persons in our lives. The whole of Christian tradition tells us that the so-called "accidental meetings" we have with individuals are not the results of pure chance, or even of a kind of "divine lottery,"[8] but gifts of divine providence and of Jesus who dwells in the midst of these encounters.

Happily, there exists a variety of forms of friendship and degrees of intensity within these friendships. There are friendships between lay persons, who are single but open to the possibility of marriage. There is the friendship between wife and husband. There are the friendships of individuals who have freely chosen to live as celibates, in imitation of Jesus in his celibacy. There are friendships between members of these various groups. Jesus dwells within these friendships and, through his example and the interior gift of agape, he calls the individuals in these friendships to grow in the love of one another, to look beyond their particular friendship to a fostering of the love of the neighbor, the spread of the kingdom, and growth in the love of God.

I would like now to focus, first, on the friendship of spouses for one another in Christ and then on the friendships of those who have chosen to be celibate, as a way of following Christ in his celibate vocation. These reflections should also shed some light on the qualities of the friendships of single persons.

Certain questions arise, however, which all friends, whether married or not, should ask about each of their particular friendships. Is Jesus a "third" in our friendship? Are we awed by Jesus' promise to be present wherever two or more are together in his name? Does the indwelling presence of Jesus in our friendship affect the quality of the type of friendship we enjoy? Does our friendship, in Aelred's words, "begin in Christ and continue in Christ"? Does our friendship dispose us to be more friendly and loving toward others? Finally, do we strive with the help of

Jesus' Holy Spirit to see that our friendship will "be perfected in Christ"?

Married Friendship in Christ

Francis de Sales writes that "in marriage there is communication of life, work, goods, affection, and indissoluble fidelity and therefore married friendship is true, holy friendship."[9] Lonergan observes that "conjugal love is to be a pure and holy love"[10] and that husband and wife are called to advance together through the daily practice of virtue and in charity toward God and neighbor. Marriage has its beginnings in the attraction of sexual desire and eros, but friendship gradually develops and the gift of agape places human friendship within the context of friendship with God. Actually, the mutual delight of the human spouses in one another disposes them to be more appreciative of the gift of friendship with Christ. Inversely, the contemplation by the spouses of the qualities of Christ as friend refines and enriches them in their human friendship with one another.

Lonergan comments that "Christian parents are the representatives . . . of Christ and his bride, the church, and so they generate children to have them regenerated in Christ."[11] Lonergan stresses the crucial role that parents have in the education of their children. He warns that human beings experience the temptation to center an "infinite craving," the craving for God, "on a finite object or release: that may be wealth, or fame, or power . . . [or] sex."[12] Christian parents, accordingly, are called to teach their children, especially by personal example, that they do not themselves put their primary emphasis on becoming wealthy, powerful, famous, but rather on loving God and one's neighbor, especially the neighbor who is most needy: the hungry, the imprisoned, the homeless, the naked, the sick, the tortured, the dying.

An Affective and Effective Love

Married Christians are clearly called, through Christ dwelling within them, to grow not only in an affective love of each other and of their children, but in an effective love—a love that proves itself by deeds. They are called to love with the love of agape and to "strive with God's help to attain the very summit of Christian perfection."[13]

The love of Christian spouses is a sacrificial love that seeks the common good of the family, but also reaches out to embrace the neighbor. This love of charity, of friendship in Christ, is tested by daily life in common; it is heightened by the responsibility for children; it is deepened by trials faced together; it is purified in the autumnal "serenity of old age, when perforce the self becomes selfless as the field of enjoyment contracts to joy in the enjoyment of others, in the romping vitality of grandchildren."[14] But this love of Christian spouses also reaches beyond love for each other, beyond love for the family, to a concern for the neighbor and for all of humankind.

It is the very nature of agape to shift one's spiritual center of gravity away from oneself and one's immediate family toward the love and service of others. Those married persons then will be happiest, as they grow old, who have sought during their lives together to inspire in their children a friendship with Christ and a desire to love as Christ loves. Those married couples will be "best friends in Christ" who have striven to make of their marriage "a series of steps upward through love of one's neighbor to the love of God."[15]

Friendships of Celibates in Christ

For centuries saints and theologians have debated about what kinds of friendship are appropriate for those Christians who have made vows or promises of perpetual celibacy and live together in community with others who have made a similar commitment. As I read the lives of female and male saints who were members of religious communities, I find that many of these saints enjoyed very close friendships with members of their own communities and often with others outside their communities. Saint Ignatius of Loyola, for example, is well known for the depth of affection in his friendship with Francis Xavier, and Teresa of Avila's letters are filled with highly moving expressions of friendship for the Carmelite priest, Jeronimo Gracian. But Jesus always abides as the "third" within these friendships and as their deepest bond.

Today, due in part to the insights of psychology, there is an emphasis in religious orders on the importance of friendship in personal development. Individuals who vow themselves to perpetual celibacy are expected to be able to relate well affectively to members of both their own and the opposite sex. Here it is worthwhile to sum up some observations of Steven Sundborg about heterosexual celibate friendship. I am drawing on his study of the psycho-spiritual development of the Carmelite sister who writes under the pen name Ruth Burrows. Sundborg's reflections are also applicable, in varying degrees, to close celibate friendships between members of the same sex.

Sundborg, articulating Burrows' experience in psychologist Rollo May's categories, stresses that the more unique and intimate a chaste friendship between two celibates is, the more agape must be at work in the friendship. Where the pull of eros is strong, agape is required to enable the two friends to reach the state of peaceful delight in each other, which is the love of philia or natural friendship. Possessiveness needs to give way to a friendship which is confident, joyous, liberating, selfless, peaceful. Burrows states unequivocally that "the very nature" of an intimate celibate love-union is "sacrificial."[16] And it is only possible to make the necessary sacrifices if the two friends are deeply prayerful and include their friendship in their prayers. Also, most importantly, the friends should each have a third person, preferably of their own sex,[17] to whom they can be completely open about their special friendship. The relationship to a third person offers a source of objectivity about the quality of the friendship; it also "may serve a crucial role by giving the celibate a basis of affective support and love which enables him or her to face more easily the emotional sacrifices required in the development of the intimate friendship."[18]

Catherine of Siena and Raymond of Capua

The sacrificial nature of intimate celibate friendship stands out vividly in friendships such as that between Catherine of Siena and Raymond of Capua. Catherine, in a letter to Raymond, speaks of a special faith and love given by God and "belonging to those who love another more intimately, like the close and special love between us two."[19] Yet, Catherine's love for Raymond did not prevent her from urging him to undertake a dangerous mission. Moreover, she told Raymond just before he left: "Go now with God, for I feel that never again in this life will we have a long talk together like this."[20] Raymond recounts that Catherine came down to the ship on which he was to sail and, as it got underway, she knelt down, prayed and wept. Raymond then states with tender feeling: "I went away; she remained behind; and before I came back she had gone to heaven."[21]

Celibates in a close friendship also need the support of their religious communities in their friendship; and a sign of the God-given character of their friendship is that it makes them more open in love to the members of their communities, not less. Any relationship between celibates that "builds walls around the relationship and keeps others outside of it" is inauthentic because "it is obvious by the very nature of religious life that this kind of exclusivity is not acceptable and in fact is very destructive of community life."[22]

The Integration of Sexuality, Eros and Philia in Agape

Authentic friendship between celibates deepens their own personal wholeness and effects, especially through the workings of agape, an integration of sexuality, eros and philia. Such friendship expands the capacity for selfless love and enlivens the feeling life of the friends. It also reveals "what aspect of the authentic desire for love can be fulfilled through human love and what aspect of this desire can be fulfilled only by the love of God."[23] Indeed, the rich experience of the fulfilling qualities of human love inspires in each of the friends "a greater impetus to seek the total fulfillment of this desire for love in God."[24]

The human affirmation that a celibate experiences in authentic friendship "is a kind of affirmation which uniquely points toward the kind of total affirmation God's love alone can give."[25] Affirmation in friendship also makes the celibate more capable of seeking God "with his or her emotions rather than in spite of them."[26] It is, of course, in the last analysis, Jesus and the Abba who make authentic, celibate love-union possible by sending their Holy Spirit of love and the gift of agape into the hearts of the celibate friends and coming themselves to dwell there.

It is very important for all friends in Christ, whether they be celibates, married couples or single, to reflect upon the love of friendship they experience and to speak with one another about their love. Thus, Karl Rahner argues that a person in love needs to reflect on his or her love. "It is not a matter of indifference to the love itself whether or not the lover . . . reflect[s] upon it." In fact, Rahner insists, reflecting on love is part of the very growth of that love.[27] But it is not enough for the lover to reflect on his or her love in solitude—though there is a time for that. Lovers, friends need to speak about their love with one another in order to grow in their love. They also need to talk about the role Christ plays in their love-relationship.

Spiritual Conversation: The Richest "Gift of Tongues"

Happily, today many lay women and lay men, both married and single, as well as priests and members of religious orders, experience a renewed urgency to speak of their common love of God and to rejoice together in the good news of the kingdom. Consequently, a chief activity of the indwelling Jesus is to inspire, through his Holy Spirit, prayerful reflections and conversations among those gathered in his name. It is, then, not surprising that the engagement of friends of Christ, from generation to generation, in eager conversation about the good news stands out as a core characteristics of their friendship in the Lord. But spiritual conversation is an art that needs constant cultivation. It is good for married persons, celibates and others to ask themselves: When did our hearts last burn within us as we spoke about what it means to be in love with Jesus Christ? When did we last ask ourselves how our friendship contributes to the building up of the kingdom of God on earth, to the service of the poor? Do we see "spiritual conversation" as a rich source of growth or do we view it rather as an embarrassment, an exercise in sentimentality? Is not the most fundamental and richest "gift of tongues" perhaps inspired, enthusiastic conversation about what we value most in life: the spread of the kingdom, love of neighbor and, above all, love of Jesus Christ and the one who sent him?

What do the saints teach us about "spiritual conversation"? Celebrated friendships in Christ of the first few hundred years include those of Gregory and Macrina his sister, whom Gregory called "the teacher";[28] John Chrysostom and Olympias, Chrysostom's adviser and defender, as well as friend and comforter;[29] Jerome and Paula, who worked with each other in Bethlehem and formed the deepest bonds of affection;[30] and two friendships where the role of conversation shines forth with a special beauty, those of Augustine and his mother Monica and Scholastica and her brother, Benedict.

Monica and Augustine

Saint Augustine was estranged from his mother during a significant portion of his life, but in the final period of Monica's life, she and her son grew very close together in a deep and holy friendship. Augustine in his *Confessions* recounts a special moment he and his mother shared, not long before she died. He writes that "it came to pass . . . that she and I stood alone, leaning in a certain

window, which looked into the garden of the house . . . at Ostia";
"we were discoursing then together, alone, very sweetly"; "we
were enquiring between ourselves in the presence of the Truth,
which Thou art, of what sort the eternal life of the saints was to be,
which eye hath not seen"; "we . . . did by degrees pass through
all things . . . that we might arrive at that region of never-failing
plenty . . . where life is the Wisdom by whom all these thing are
made"; "and while we were discoursing and panting after her
[Wisdom], we slightly touched on her with the whole effort of our
heart; and we sighed and there we leave [left] bound the first fruits
of the Spirit; and returned to vocal expressions of our mouth,
where the word spoken has beginning and end."[31] This text offers
eloquent witness to the exquisite friendship in Christ that existed
between Saint Monica and her son and the quality of their spiritual
conversations.

Scholastica and Benedict

Saint Gregory recounts an incident in the lives of Saint Benedict
and his sister, Saint Scholastica, that shows the preeminent value
and role of spiritual conversation in friendship. But this time the
friendship is not that of mother and son, but of sister and brother.
Gregory tells us that Benedict and his sister used to come together
once a year, from their respective monasteries. On one occasion,
after Benedict and his sister had spent the whole day conversing
together and Benedict was about to leave for his monastery, Scholastica asked her brother to remain so that they could talk until the
morning about "the joys of the heavenly life." Benedict replied to
his sister that he could not remain outside the monastery through
the night. It was a clear evening. But, upon hearing her brother's
response, Scholastica clasped her hands together, bowed her head
and prayed. At once the crack of thunder was heard and continual
showers of rain fell. Benedict said to his sister: "What is this you
have done?" She replied: "I prayed you to stay and you would not
hear me; I prayed to Almighty God and He heard me!" Gregory
tells us that "thus it fell out that they spent the night in watching,
and received full content in spiritual discourse of heavenly matters." Gregory observes that Scholastica won out over her
brother's objections because "she had long desired to see her
brother," and since "God is charity," "with good reason she was
more powerful who loved more."[32] Saint Scholastica died not long
after this meeting with her brother and Benedict had her buried in

the tomb he had prepared for himself. So, as Gregory remarks, "it fell out, that as their minds were always one in God, so also their bodies were not separated in their burial."[33]

The gentle and wise monk Aelred of Rievaulx, writing at the request of Bernard of Clairvaux, shows how the theme of holy conversation among friends of Christ remained a constant as the centuries passed. Aelred writes of what a joy it is "to have the consolation of someone's affection—someone to whom one is deeply united by the bonds of love . . . someone whose conversation is as sweet as a song in the tedium of our daily life."[34] He tells his monks that "whoever finds enjoyment in the love of a friend, let him enjoy him in the Lord," and that to enjoy a friend in the Lord is to enjoy him "in wisdom" because Christ is Wisdom.[35] Aelred is exquisite in his gentleness and humanity. He says that with one's friends "we can share the burdens of our daily lives, and the hope of our future happiness . . . we can share our secret thoughts and strive together in our longing for the sight of Jesus' face."[36]

Ignatius of Loyola and His Companions

Javier Osuna, in his book *Friends in the Lord*, shows the central role of spiritual conversations among Saint Ignatius of Loyola (1491–1556) and his first companions in the formation of the Society of Jesus. Peter Faber, who was to become, with Francis Xavier, one of the closest friends of Ignatius, remarked how in early meetings among a small number, attracted by Ignatius, "conversation on material things swiftly gave way to spiritual conversation."[37] Osuna, citing numerous historical sources, shows how the early companions constantly nourished their friendship in Christ "in communication of all their affairs and of their inmost thoughts."[38] Jesus Christ formed the center of their common friendship[39] and thus at the point where "the group gives itself a name, their gaze is turned on Jesus" and they choose to be "the Society of Jesus, a group of friends, at Christ's disposition, to *serve* him."[40]

Francis de Sales (1567–1622), one of the most amiable of saints, in his celebrated work *Introduction to the Devout Life*, writes that for friendship to exist, there must be mutual love, awareness of reciprocal affection, and communication.[41] He stresses that "the love based on the most exquisite communication is the best"[42] and that "all other friendships are mere shadows" in comparison to the "friendship by which two, three, or more . . . share with one another their devotion and spiritual affections and establish a single spirit among themselves."[43] And what is at the core of the communication among friends? In his equally celebrated work *The Love of God* Francis answers this question when he writes: "Jesus Christ is our love; and our love is the life of our souls."[44]

Stephen Sundborg, in the study I referred to earlier, reveals the importance of spiritual conversation today in the life of a person totally dedicated to the quest of the kingdom of God. Based on conversations with Sister Ruth Burrows and the study of her writings, Sundborg shows the profound role that Ruth's friendships with a priest called "John" and a Carmelite sister, Elsa, have played and continue to play in her psychological and spiritual development. Sundborg points out, in the context of Ruth's spiritual conversations with Elsa, that "Ruth's lifelong desire to be understood especially in the darkness of her spiritual way is fulfilled" and "is of immeasurable help in her understanding of her transforming union and in her becoming an important writer in our day on prayer and the mystical life."[45] And Ruth Burrows herself reveals the depth of Jesus' loving presence in her own life when she writes toward the conclusion of her commentary on St. Teresa of Avila's *Interior Castle:*

> The fundamental grace of entry into the mystical states is that Jesus becomes our Jesus. We begin to grope into the fathomless caverns of Jesus. . . . We see life, reality, everything in terms of him. His is the face always present in our consciousness. . . . We are becoming Jesus. No question about it but that there will be sheer avidity to know all we can of him, to seek the linaments of his beloved face in the gospels, and always we shall find him more and more.[46]

The Holy Rhythm in Loving Christ and the Neighbor

Spiritual conversation also leads us to ever deeper knowledge of Jesus; it is often born of prayer and leads in turn to more prayer, as well as to the performance of works of mercy in the service of one's neighbor. Indeed, a key proof of Jesus' abiding presence in the holy friendships with which he blesses us is, as it were, the graceful rhythm by which we move from a focus in prayer on a human friend to a faith-encounter with Jesus himself. Aelred of Rievaulx recounts how in praying to Christ on behalf of a friend it sometimes happens that "quickly and imperceptibly the one love passes over into the other, and coming, as it were, into close contact with . . . Christ himself, the friend begins to taste his sweetness and to experience his charm."[47] Some might find Aelred's language a bit too "sweet" for modern taste, but the insight that his words convey remains as valid today as it was a thousand years ago.

In yet another passage, Aelred affirms the holy rhythm whereby the love of a friend in Christ lifts us up to the love of Jesus, and from this encounter we descend again to the love of friend and neighbor. In speaking of one of his most treasured friends Aelred writes:

> He was the refuge of my spirit, the sweet solace of my griefs, whose heart of love received me when fatigued from labors, whose counsel refreshed me when plunged in sadness and grief. He himself calmed me when distressed, he soothed me when angry. Whenever anything unpleasant occurred, I referred it to him, so that, shoulder to shoulder, I was able to bear more easily what I could not bear alone.[48]

Aelred then asks himself: "Was it not a foretaste of blessedness thus to love and thus to be loved . . . and in this way from the sweetness of fraternal charity to wing one's flight aloft . . . and by the ladder of charity now to mount to the embrace of Christ himself; and again to descend to the love of neighbor."[49] No text reveals in a more touching manner the reality of the indwelling presence of Jesus in holy friendships. If we love Jesus authentically in our friends, whom we see, then Jesus will touch us and reveal himself to us in unexpected and joyous ways. We, in turn, will be reinvigorated in our desire to embrace and serve Jesus, especially in the poorest of the poor, for he has identified himself with them in a love of preference and befriends them most of all.

"I Say to My Beloved: You Shall Never Die"

Finally, one of the most urgent longings of friendship in its richest forms is that it perdure. Philosopher Gabriel Marcel somewhere says: "I say to my beloved: You shall never die." In the gospel of John Jesus tells his close friend Martha, who is grieving over the death of her brother Lazarus: "I am the resurrection and the life; he who believes in me, though he die, yet shall he live, and whoever lives and believes in me shall never die. Do you believe this?'' (Jn 11:25–26).

Psychologist Erik Erikson in his description of eight stages in human development suggests that, in a healthy growth process, a person in the last four stages of maturation achieves, respectively, a solid sense of personal identity, a capacity for true intimacy, a productive care for the future of family and humankind, and an inner integrity, whereby the individual is at peace within and reconciled to the prospect of dying. Erikson names these last four stages, in their positive forms, as identity, intimacy, generativity, integrity. He says that the qualities and virtues that correspond, respectively, to these last four stages are devotion and fidelity, affiliation and love, production and care, renunciation and wisdom.[50]

Our reflections on the friendships of holy people with Jesus and with one another in Jesus reveal, by and large, the presence in God's holy ones of the virtues of fidelity, love, care and wisdom. Of course, the saints too have their flaws, developmental inadequacies, imperfections. But for the Christian believer death is not the end of friendship with Jesus or with those who love Jesus. Friendships purdure in a purified, intensified, transfigured form in the resurrection from the dead. Accordingly, the reconciliation of the holy ones with death is not fatalistic, but full of hope. In the words of Gerard Manley Hopkins, taken from his *The Leaden Echo and the Golden Echo:*

See; not a hair is, not an eyelash, not the least lash lost; every
    hair is, hair of the head, numbered.

. . .

O then, weary then why should we tread? O why are we so
    haggard at the heart, so care-coiled, care-killed

. . .

When the thing we freely forfeit is kept
    with fonder a care,
Fonder a care kept than we could have kept it, kept
Far with fonder a care

. . .

Where kept? Do but tell us where kept, where.—
Yonder.—What high as that! We follow, now we follow.—.
    Yonder, yes yonder, yonder,
Yonder.[51]

Francis Xavier, as he set out on his journey to India, wrote to Ignatius and his other brothers and friends in Rome: "We beg. . . . you . . . again and again in the Lord, through our most intimate friendship in Christ Jesus, to advise us in writing on the means you think we should follow there [in India] so as to serve our Lord God better."[52] Francis ends his letter with an expression of friendship that is suffused with fidelity, love, care, wisdom:

> We have nothing more to write to you from here except that we are ready to sail. We conclude with the request that our Lord Christ may give us the favor of seeing each other and of being physically united with each other again in the other life; for I do not know if we shall ever see each other again in this life, not only because of the great distance from Rome to India, but also because of the great harvest which waits for us there without our having to go elsewhere to look for it. Whoever goes first to the other life and does not find his brother there whom he loves in the Lord should ask Christ our Lord to unite us all there in His glory.[53]

"We Shall Always Be with the Lord"

From New Testament times Christians expressed concern about the fate of their friends, their brother and sister believers, who had died. Paul, in his first epistle to the Thessalonians, makes it clear to the Christian community that they should not grieve, in the way pagans do, about their loved ones who have died. Paul tells them that God, who raised Jesus from the dead, will also raise up, through Jesus, those who have died. He ends by saying that in the final resurrection "we shall always be with the Lord" and that therefore the Thessalonians should comfort one another with these words (1 Thes 4:17–18).

Gerard Manley Hopkins, in his sonnet *The Lantern Out of Doors,* poignantly laments the passing from our lives—either through physical separation or death—of persons with rare gifts of beauty of one type or other. Hopkins notes the proverbial truth that "out of sight is out of mind." But then the poet's spirit gladdens at the thought that "Christ minds," that Christ shows ongoing concern for these persons:

> Christ minds; Christ's interest, what to avow or amend
>   There, eyes them, heart wants, care haunts,
>   foot follows kind,

Their ransom, their rescue, and first, fast,
    last friend.[54]

Aelred, in his final reflections on friendship, tells his friend
Walter that, although here on earth we can only enjoy very intimate friendships with a few, in heaven the gift of friendship will be
extended to everyone. Aelred says: "This friendship, to which
here we admit but few, will be outpoured upon all and by all
outpoured upon God, and God shall be all in all."[55]

Nor should we in any way fear that our friends will somehow
fade away and vanish when God becomes "all in all." In the mystical vision of Saint Ignatius "there is no smothering of creation in
the presence of the all-overwhelming Trinitarian God."[56] Indeed,
Teilhard de Chardin insists that "Christianity alone . . . saves
. . . the essential aspiration of all mysticism: to be united (that is,
to become the other) while remaining oneself." Chardin insists
that "we can only lose ourselves in God by prolonging the most
individual characteristics of beings far beyond themselves: that is
the fundamental rule by which we can always distinguish the true
mystic from his counterfeits."[57] This means that in heaven friends
do not vanish into the Absolute that is God; rather, each friend
reveals in herself or himself a unique facet of the Beauty that is
God. As Augustine puts it so succinctly: "This is our highest re-
ward, that we should fully enjoy Him, and that all who enjoy Him
should enjoy one another in Him."[58]

Recently, Anne Carr has recommended that there is a most
special value today in imaging God as friend. She urges that, far
from the sentimentality that such a homely image might suggest,
there is a desperate need precisely for the categories of friend and
friendship. To envisage God as friend, she says, would be to understand God as "friend to humankind as a whole, and even more
intimately as friend to every individual and every nation and every
group in its particularities." Carr notes that "Jesus' relationship to
his disciples, as the Gospel stories describe it, was that of chosen
friends" and that "friendship transformed the lives of those disciples—both women and men—in ways beyond their wildest imagining as the Spirit pressed them forward."[59]

Aelred of Rievaulx certainly provides a most solid foundation in
Christian tradition for imaging God in the categories of friend and
friendship. If, then, there is basic validity in Aelred's celebrated
affirmation that "God is Friendship," we cannot do much better
than to enter into friendship with Jesus, who is God's loving kind-

ness (Tit 3:4) dwelling in our midst. Then together with Jesus, our beloved Wisdom-friend, we can make our way, guided by his Holy Spirit of love, into the very depths of the heart of the God who is friendship.

Notes

1. Aelred of Rievaulx, *Spiritual Friendship*, translated by Mary Laker (Washington D.C.: Cistercian Publications Consortium Press, 1974), p. 51.

2. Ibid., p. 53.

3. Maurice Henry-Couannier, *Saint Francis de Sales and His Friends*, translated by Veronica Morrow (Staten Island: Alba House, 1964), p. 172.

4. Michael de la Bedoyere, *Francois de Sales* (New York: Harper & Brothers, 1960), p. 125.

5. Georges Guitton, *Perfect Friend*, translated by William Young (St. Louis: B. Herder Book Co., 1956), p. 141.

6. Ibid., p. 142.

7. Bernard Tyrrell, *Christotherapy II* (New York: Paulist Press, 1982), p. 222.

8. Gilbert Meilaender, *Friendship: A Study in Theological Ethics* (Notre Dame: Notre Dame Press, 1981), p. 20.

9. Francis de Sales, *Introduction to the Devout Life*, translated by John Ryan (Garden City, New York: Doubleday, 1972), p. 170.

10. Bernard Lonergan, "Finality, Love, Marriage," *Collection* (New York: Herder and Herder, 1967), p. 27.

11. Ibid., p. 48.

12. Ibid., p. 50.

13. Ibid., p. 27.

14. Ibid., p. 37.

15. Ibid., p. 45.

16. Cited by Stephen Sundborg, *Sexual-Affective Integration in Celibacy* (Rome: Gregorian University Press, 1984) p. 83.

17. Ibid.

18. Ibid., pp. 83–84.

19. Cited by Mary Ann Fatula, "Catherine of Siena on the Communion of Friendship," *Review for Religious*, 43, 1984, p. 228.

20. Raymond of Capua, *The Life of Catherine of Siena*, translated by Conleth Kearns (Wilmington: Michael Glazier, 1980), p. 313.

21. Ibid.

22. Steven Sundborg, p. 88.

23. Ibid., p. 94.

24. Ibid., p. 95.

25. Ibid., p. 96.

26. Ibid., p. 95.

27. Karl Rahner, "The Development of Doctrine," *Theological Investigations I,* translated by Cornelius Ernst (Baltimore: Helicon Press, 1965), p. 64.

28. Cited by Rosemary Rader, *Breaking Boundaries: Male/Female Friendship in Early Christian Communities* (New York: Paulist Press, 1983), p. 89.

29. Ibid., p. 98.

30. Ibid., pp. 99–103.

31. Augustine, *The Confessions of St. Augustine,* translated by Edward B. Pusey (New York: Pocket Books, 1957), pp. 164–165.

32. T. F. Lindsay, *Saint Benedict: His Life and Work* (London: Burns & Oates, 1949), pp. 174–175.

33. Ibid., pp. 174–177.

34. Aelred of Rievaulx, *The Mirror of Charity,* translated by Geoffrey Webb and Adrian Walker (London: A. R. Mowbray, 1962), p. 139.

35. Ibid., p. 140.

36. Ibid., p. 141.

37. Javier Osuna, *Friends in the Lord,* translated by Nicolas King (Exeter: Catholic Records Press, 1974), p. 48.

38. Ibid., p. 61.

39. Ibid., p. 143.

40. Ibid., p. 81.

41. Francis de Sales, *Introduction to the Devout Life,* p. 169.

42. Ibid., p. 170.

43. Ibid., p. 175.

44. Francis de Sales, *The Love of God,* translated by Vincent Kerns (Westminster, Maryland: Newman Press, 1962), p. 289.

45. Stephen Sundborg, *Sexual-Affective Integration in Celibacy,* p. 18.

46. Ruth Burrows, *Fire Upon The Earth: Interior Castle Explored* (Denville, New Jersey: Dimension Books, 1981), p. 108.

47. Aelred of Rievaulx, *Spiritual Friendship,* p. 131.

48. Ibid., p. 129.

49. Ibid.

50. Erik H. Erikson, *Childhood and Society* (New York: W.W. Norton, 1963), p. 274.

51. Gerard Manley Hopkins, *Gerard Manley Hopkins,* selection of poems with introduction and notes by W.H. Gardner (Baltimore: Penguin Books, 1958), p. 54.

52. Georg Schurhammer, *Francis Xavier: His Life, His Time, I,* translated by M. Joseph Costelloe), p. 718.

53. Ibid., p. 719.

54. Gerard Manley Hopkins, *Gerard Manley Hopkins,* p. 29.

55. Aelred, *Spiritual Friendship,* p. 132.

56. Adolf Haas, "The Mysticism of St. Ignatius According to His *Spiri-*

tual Diary," *Ignatius of Loyola: His Personality and Spiritual Heritage* (St. Louis: The Institute of Jesuit Sources, 1977), p. 175.

57. Cited by Michael Cox, *Handbook of Christian Spirituality* (New York: Harper and Row, 1985), p. 242.

58. Cited by Maria Josephine McErlane, "Friendship According to St. Augustine," *Review for Religious* 41, 1982, p. 603.

59. Anne Carr, *Transforming Grace* (San Francisco: Harper and Row, 1988), p. 213.